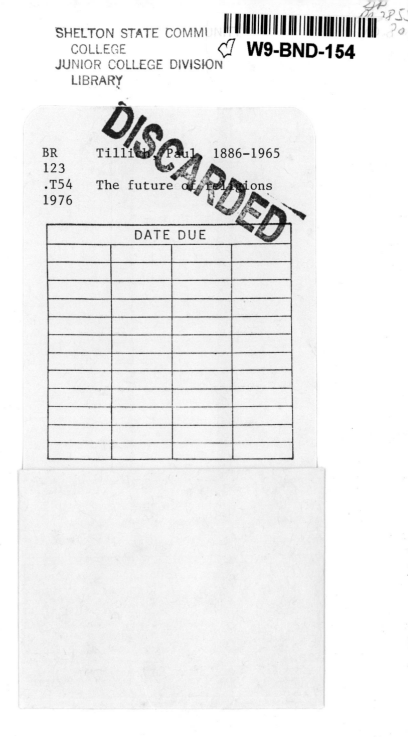

DATE DUE

THE FUTURE
OF RELIGIONS

Edited by Jerald C. Brauer

THE FUTURE
OF RELIGIONS

  Paul Tillich

GREENWOOD PRESS, PUBLISHERS
WESTPORT, CONNECTICUT

Library of Congress Cataloging in Publication Data

Tillich, Paul, 1886-1965.
   The future of religions.

      Reprint of the ed. published by Harper & Row,
New York.
      CONTENTS: Tributes to Paul Tillich: Brauer,
J. C. Paul Tillich's impact on America. Pauck, W.
The sources of Paul Tillich's richness. Eliade, M.
Paul Tillich and the history of religions. [etc.]
      1. Christianity--20th century--Addresses, es-
says, lectures. 2. Tillich, Paul, 1886-1965--
Addresses, essays, lectures. I. Brauer, Jerald C.
II. Title.
[BR123.T54 1976]   230'.092'4   76-7566
ISBN 0-8371-8861-X

"Frontiers" by Paul Tillich is reprinted from *The Journal of Bible and Religion*, Vol. XXXIII, No. 1 (January, 1965). Copyright 1965 by the American Academy of Religion. Translated by Franklin Littell. Used by permission of the publisher. "The Sources of Paul Tillich's Richness" by Wilhelm Pauck is reprinted from *Union Seminary Quarterly Review*, Vol. XXI, No. 1 (November, 1965). Used by permission of the publisher.

Originally published in 1966 by Harper & Row, Publishers, New York

Reprinted with the permission of Harper & Row, Publishers, Inc.

Reprinted in 1976 by Greenwood Press, Inc., 51 Riverside Avenue, Westport, Conn. 06880

Library of Congress catalog card number 76-7566
ISBN 0-8371-8861-X

Printed in the United States of America

10 9 8 7 6 5 4 3 2

ᴨᴗᴨᴗᴨᴗ *Contents*

Photographs by Archie Lieberman follow page 32

ERRATUM

On page 11, line 16 down, please read:

Thanks is extended to Stanley Grean, Associate Professor of Philosophy, Ohio University, who edited the tape of the lecture on "The Decline and the Validity of the Idea of Progress," delivered on May 19, 1964, as one in the series of The Edwin and Ruth Kennedy Lectures at Ohio University, Athens, Ohio.

~~~~~~~~~~ *Editor's Preface*

On the evening of October 12, 1965, Paul Tillich presented a public lecture entitled "The Significance of the History of Religions for the Systematic Theologian." It was the concluding lecture in a conference on history of religions held by his colleagues of the Divinity School of The University of Chicago. Tillich spent two years in a joint seminar with Mircea Eliade, and so it was natural that he should be asked to deliver this lecture. The audience demonstrated its enthusiasm by loud and sustained applause. At four o'clock the next morning Paul Tillich suffered a severe heart attack, and ten days later he died. Thus, the lecture represents his last public words.

The lecture was delivered by Tillich from ten pages of carefully outlined notes, and it proved to be one of his most tightly packed and comprehensive lectures of recent years. Obviously it represents a major effort to deal with what he felt was a subject of urgent importance. Though it in no way contradicts his basic orientation, neither is it merely a series of deductions from his system. It is a fresh and vigorous effort to outline the major presuppositions, problems, and future directions of what he clearly felt was the next stage for systematic theology.

Tillich pointed out that his own systematic theology was written for a specific purpose and before his work with Eliade. As a consequence of his two years' work in depth in history of religions, Tillich saw the possibility of a new type of systematic theology in which an interpretation of Christian theology would be developed in dialogue with the insights of the other religions or in relation to a "different fragmentary manifestation of theonomy . . ." He specifically stated that "This is my hope for the future of theology."

In the lecture, Tillich brought under cogent criticism both orthodoxy, new and old, and also the so-called "God is dead" theologians.

7

He accused both of a reductionism that is destructive for theology. The former is unable to locate revelation anywhere except in the Christ event and cannot properly value the secular. The latter rejects all possibility of confronting the specifically divine at the depths of the secular yet seeks to make Jesus somehow entirely unique or especially significant for secular culture. They find no way of differentiating between the "merely secular" and "that secular which would be the object of a secular theology."

Neither of these views can be concerned with or be creatively related to the religious experiences of mankind or to the history of religions; therefore, neither of them represents the future of theology as seen by Tillich. The very term "religion" still causes problems for the systematic theologian, and that problem is intensified by an unwitting but nevertheless real alliance between the two fronts of resistance to religion—the orthodox and the secular. Tillich is equally critical of that form of reductionism that would seek the common elements in all religions in a fruitless search for the truly religious. Such an attempt is as destructive of the genuinely religious as are the orthodox and the secular.

Over against these other views, Tillich proposes what he calls a "dynamic typological" approach that seeks to discover the particular and the unique manifestations of the holy within a given religion. These manifestations involve certain elements wherever the Holy is experienced; however, these elements occur in different relationships and in varying intensity in particular religions. He sees the true *telos* of all religion in a unity of these special elements whose aim is to become a "Religion of the Concrete Spirit." Though no religion can be identified with this historically, all religions approximate this reality more or less, and in fragmentary ways it has been and is being realized in history. It is at this point that Tillich indicates a new possibility for a Christological approach which relates Christianity to other religions and reopens the question of the relation of Christianity to the secular.

It is clear why Tillich hoped the future of Christian theology would develop out of an intensive dialectic between systematic theological study and religious historical studies. One can assume that Tillich intended this to take place between committed scholars from the various religions. It is interesting to note that at the very moment Christian theology is beginning to develop in a new context of dialogue between

Roman Catholics and Protestants and in a new relationship to the secular, that at this moment Tillich saw its future in the next and widest circle—its relation to the world's great religions past and present.

Paul Tillich was convinced that the secular cannot, by definition and in reality, live by itself. That is why he was a theologian, and that is why he believed and argued that religion would never pass away. He was fully secular in fighting against the domination of life by the historical manifestations of the Holy, but he was fully religious in proclaiming the divine depth of the secular in the face of its threatened emptiness. Thus, his last lecture appears as prophetic as his earliest work. Unfortunately he had opportunity only to sketch out directions, but so incisive and thorough is his initial sketch that it provides insight and resources for those who will inevitably move in this direction.

It is appropriate to include with this lecture several other lectures of his last years. Each in its own way complements the main thrust of the "History of Religions" lecture. Each demonstrates his concern with the major issues of our epoch and reflects the continuity of his thought. "Frontiers" was his address delivered in Frankfurt on the occasion of his reception of the Peace Prize of the German Book Trade in 1962. In it he sketched out in new dimensions one of his basic themes— what it means for an individual and for nations to live on the boundary. Among the many points he makes, two are of special interest in relation to his last lecture.

Nobody was more aware of the dangers of "culture-Christianity" than was Paul Tillich. He experienced and fought the demonic absorbtion of Christianity by German culture in Hitler's Germany, and he recognized the necessity of the churches drawing into their tradition to preserve their identity even at the cost of narrowing their boundary. Today the situation is different, and he called for the churches to return to the frontier of culture and "to cross over it and wrestle for the Beyond in the to-and-fro between church and culture." Ever alert to changes in history, Tillich clearly saw the new challenge and called upon the Church to risk itself in the effort to be relevant to numerous people who though not in the churches belong to them essentially. Thus, he saw the Church in a new frontier situation. Also he saw all religions playing a role in the boundary situation in that all religions can witness to the reality of the infinite crossing the boundary of the finite. All religions can be important from this point of view, both for nations and for individuals.

His lecture on "The Effects of Space Exploration on Man's Condition and Stature" is a perfect illustration of Tillich's profound concern with man's humanity and of Tillich's uncanny ability to probe the most recent secular achievements of man. One of his remarkable gifts was his ability to see all central issues of modern man from a religious or a theological perspective. Space exploration and its consequences is a perfect case in point. His analysis of the situation reflects a remarkable appreciation for the necessity and the achievements of the "horizontal" perspective on life which now culminates in the first steps of space exploration. Tillich correctly senses this perspective and its consequences as the creator of a new set of symbols that present modern man with a new ideal of human existence. But he also puts his sensitive finger on the problem which arises in the center of the new ideal—the problem of how man will remain essentially human in the space age. Again he warns that the secular cannot live on secularity alone. Man will be driven to the genuine religious depth or to the quasi-religious creations of the secular itself.

The lecture on "The Decline and the Validity of the Idea of Progress" was delivered in the spring of 1964, and it illustrates the openness of Tillich to the shift in sentiment on the part of modern man. He correctly stated that "today we need a new inquiry into the validity and the limits of the idea of progress." Having buried a somewhat naïve concept of progressivistic development, America soon developed a sophistication and realism that has led many to the brink of cynicism. This is especially dangerous in a nation with world-wide responsibilities in an atomic age, and doubly difficult for individuals living in a highly impersonal technological society. Modern Americans and modern man desperately need a view of history that is at once open to the future yet realistic in its aspirations. Again Tillich sees religion as one force providing such a perspective, particularly insofar as it involves a view of the possibilities of *kairoi*, moments of partial but highly creative fulfillment in history.

The four lectures, taken together, seek to document Tillich's vision of the "Future of Religions" for mankind. From his viewpoint there can be no future for man apart from the religious dimension and perspective. All four lectures document that basic point. It is one of those strange quirks of history that Paul Tillich ended his final lecture with this statement, "But now my last word." In his last word he dealt with the issue of the relationship between Christian systematic theology and other religions. He wanted to emphasize the centrality of the experiential basis in a particular religion yet he wished to affirm equally the search for the universal through the concrete. In the coming encounter between the world's religions he saw the possibility, on a new level, of that for which he worked his entire life, namely, "the openness to spiritual freedom both from one's own foundation and for one's own foundation."

A special word of acknowledgment must be made to Archie Lieberman who took the photographs which are so revelatory of Tillich's own being. The moods and the manifold interests of the man shine through and make manifest his ideas and concerns. For Archie Lieberman his photographing of Tillich quickly became a labor of friendship and of love. [Thanks is extended to Stanley Grean, Associate Professor of Philosophy, Ohio University, who edited the tape of the lecture on "The Decline and the Validity of the Idea of Progress," delivered on May 19, 1964, as one in the series of The Edwin and Ruth Kennedy Lectures at Ohio University, Athens, Ohio.] The lecture has not been published previously. We are grateful to the editors of *The Journal of Bible and Religion* for permission to publish the "Frontiers" article which first appeared in their journal and was translated by Professor Franklin Littell. Though Professor Tillich indicated that the lecture on "Space Exploration" was to be published in 1964, we have been unable to find it in print. The editor prepared the lecture on "History of Religions" based upon written notes and a full tape recording. The three memorial addresses were delievered at the Tillich Memorial Service of the Divinity School held in Rockefeller Memorial Chapel of the University of Chicago, October 29, 1965. Each man was instructed to deal briefly with a special facet of Tillich's life.

Gratitude is expressed to Mrs. Hannah Tillich and to Dr. Robert C. Kimball, Executor of the Estate of Paul Tillich, for furnishing some of the manuscripts and permitting their use in this book.

JERALD C. BRAUER
Dean and Professor of Church History

The Divinity School, The University of Chicago

Tributes to Paul Tillich

~~~~~ *Paul Tillich's*

Impact on America – JERALD C. BRAUER

PAUL TILLICH stood alone as the interpreter of Christian faith
to American culture and as one of the few theologians who could
speak to the entire modern world so it would listen. It is one
matter to speak to the world; it is quite another matter to be taken
seriously. Tillich was taken seriously both by those who disagreed
with him and by those who agreed with him. His books were
read by countless thousands, impossible demands were made on
him as a lecturer, his concepts were commonplace at cocktail
parties, he was quoted and interviewed constantly by all media of
mass communication, and he was listened to gladly by students,
which was for him a great source of joy. With no publicity to speak
of, seven thousand students turned out to hear him at the University of California, Berkeley, only a few months before his death.

Tillich's impact on students was obvious, overwhelming, and
enduring. Why was this so? What made Paul Tillich so special
in his appeal to American students? No full explanation is possible,
and these brief lines make no pretense at a coldly objective analysis.
Nevertheless, it is possible on the part of those of us who worked
closely with him over the years to offer explanations out of our
observation and participation. To be sure, such an analysis will
be colored by love and affection, though in no sense blinded.

Paul Tillich was a great teacher and not simply a great scholar
and author. But how does one fathom the secret of an unusual
teacher? Some will argue that Tillich had an extraordinary charis-

matic personality that mesmerized students and all audiences. His slow, steady, and at times ponderous, delivery was aided by just enough of a German accent to intrigue and to edify. Undoubtedly, Tillich had a lecture style that was his own, but his appeal was not based on that. He was but one among many German émigré professors who lectured in that fashion.

He had a charisma, but it was not dependent upon his lecture style. In fact it was his charisma that was shining through his style, and made it endearing and effective. It was the man who made the style, and not the style that made the man. His unpretentiousness, absolute honesty, courage, love of people and ideas manifested themselves through his lectures. In spite of his profound learning and keen mind, there was a childlike quality that came through. Tillich's lectures probably revealed more of his own being than do the lectures of most professors. This was also sensed by students, and they responded accordingly.

Charisma alone cannot account for the impact of Paul Tillich on students. Perhaps most important was his sheer power of mind. Nobody could hear Tillich lecture without coming away amazed at the quality of the man's mind. One was constantly struck by the rich resource of classical training, the liberally furnished store of knowledge and wisdom, the depth and breadth of reading and of perception. Never was this vast knowledge disconnected or random. It was thoroughly organized in a disciplined fashion and cogently related to key issues.

Paul Tillich's analytic powers in theology and philosophy were beautiful to behold. They were an artistic achievement. Sitting with me one evening, he sketched out for my reaction the outline of an article about which he had been thinking for some time. As he worked out the major concepts, their interrelationships, and their culmination, it was like listening to a beautiful fugue unfold. How often students heard him deliver a lecture that could be described only as a virtuoso completing an intricate solo. Students had the feeling that his mind was creating before their very eyes. Frequently it was.

Paul Tillich had the unusual combination of a powerfully analytic mind yet a constructive or creative mind. The power of analysis was never used simply for its own sake—to analyze the ideas of other men or of other periods of history. His primary task was always to construct his own system, to create his vision of meaning and coherence. This was one of the most compelling forces that attracted and held the attention of students. Finely honed analytic minds are commonplace in universities, but a synthetic mind, a truly constructive or creative mind is a rarity. Modern man may reject and criticize the few attempts made to construct systems or syntheses, but such attempts are always admired and carefully scrutinized.

The real secret of Paul Tillich's appeal for students lies in the fact that he needed them. Without his students, he was incomplete. Students were not something to be endured, the teaching of whom was a necessary obligation of an academic contract. He lived in and through students. On them he tested out his ideas. To them he offered his insights and experience. He brought to students an absolute honesty and candor. There was no question sacrosanct or reserved. Their questions were his, and his questions quickly became theirs. Though he handled his lectures with a sure touch, as one who spoke from profound experience, never did Tillich condescend or cajole. He dealt honestly and openly with his students. They helped to form his thought.

It was because Tillich needed students for his own completion that they accepted him so gladly. They were wanted and needed not to build a man's ego but to participate in a process of learning that can only be complete where teacher and student genuinely need each other and contribute to each other. Teaching was for him a process of love, and so he received love in return.

It was impossible for an honest student to ask a stupid question of Paul Tillich. Any question asked honestly was picked up by him and reworked into a profound question as it was discussed by him. Some thought Tillich did this to win or impress the students. He did not have to win or impress them, they were already won and impressed. The fact was that Tillich saw implicit in all questions, however naive and stumbling, the germ of the real question for which an immature mind was grasping. When Tillich finished answering such a question the student was astonished that he had asked such a profound question. That frequently was the first step in a learning experience.

Tillich also had a deep sense of obligation to his students. In spite of one of the busiest schedules in American higher education, Paul Tillich probably missed fewer clases in his long academic career than does the average American professor in an average three year period. He used to say that this compulsion to be present for his classes was the consequence of his Prussian conscience. All who knew him, knew better. His basic desire was to be with his own class with which he always developed a special relationship. He needed them, and they needed him.

What can be said of Paul Tillich's impact on and relationship to the American scene? For twenty years he labored in his new homeland with little public recognition. He was, and in one sense he will always remain, the theologian's theologian. Suddenly, in the 1950's he burst into public view and became the most eloquent spokesman for religion in America. Some will say this was due to the publication of the first volume of his *Systematic Theology* and to the rapid appearance of a series of his works. There is some truth in that.

Probably the explanation of his sudden acceptance is to be found in the American situation itself. Prior to the end of World War II, before the appearance and intensification of post war tensions, America was not ready for or open to Tillich's type of theologizing. The postwar period provided the kairotic moment for the impact of Paul Tillich on America.

The complexity of his thought can be described in many ways. One can speak of the development of his method of correlation, his basic use of the ontological principle of being, his fresh apprehension of the significance of Jesus Christ as the New Being, or

18

his subtle and consistent use of dialectic. All of these are fundamental to his theological perspective.

Underlying the theology is the man, and he provided the key
that opens the door to understand him. He described himself as
a man who always lived on the boundary—on the boundary between the holy and the profane, on the boundary between philosophy and theology, on the boundary between religion and culture,
on the boundary between Europe and America, and on the
boundary between being and non-being. Dialectic was not an
intellectual choice for Paul Tillich; it was the consequence of his
own being.

Such a theologian was not easily understood or appreciated in
the American context. Why was such a tortuous dialectic necessary? Cannot one easily distinguish between being a theologian
and being a philosopher? Why was it not simple to define the
moral, the good, and then to do it? Why is such subtle analysis
and delicate balance necessary? One only has to seek the truth and
then define it in doing it. That was the America of the pre-atomic
age. She did not live on the boundary constantly balancing between
alternatives. America lived in a rich land relatively untouched
by the cataclysms of the world and open to a boundless future
and unlimited possibilities.

After the war, America found herself, for the first time, in the
boundary situation, and she did not like it. There are those who are
still incapable of living with it, and we call them extremists.
America fell from her Adamic period and entered the atomic age.
She was caught on the boundary between victory and the immediate appearance of an enemy. She believed herself the cham-
pion of liberty and of the rights of the people, and she found
herself drawn into the defense of the status quo. She believed
her technology would usher in a new age of peace and prosperity,
and she experienced the constant threat of atomic annihilation.
She found herself with unsought and unprecedented power, and
she was frustrated in her attempts to use it creatively. At the

height of her power and technological might, America experienced her deepest moment of insecurity. In the midst of her wealth and riches, she experienced, as never before, the threat of meaninglessness.

America was frustrated, threatened, somewhat disillusioned, and groping for answers. She was on the boundary situation for the first time in her history. It was exceedingly difficult to shift a national perspective, let alone an individual one, from the boundless to the boundary situation. It was precisely at this point that Paul Tillich's theology began to speak to the American situation. He, probably more than any single figure in America, prepared the American people to live on the boundary situation. He helped them to begin to make the transition from the situation of innocence to the necessity of realism without falling into cynicism. He did this primarily through a religious vision, but it was a vision that embraced every aspect of life—the personal and the social, the political and the cultural. This is why millions of Americans read and heard Tillich so gladly. Living on the boundary for the first time, they turned to one whose life and theology was worked out on the boundary.

Undoubtedly some will say that Tillich is the last of a certain kind of theologian, or that, in a sense, he was a throwback to a type of theologian who no longer exists. To them he represents the passing of an epoch. He is to be admired but more as a museum piece than as a theologian. This can be said only if we assume that the primary goal of a systematic theology is to create disciples who repeat the system, or if the goal is to provide the basis on which all knowledge is systematized from a single consistent theological point of view. What if these are not the goals of a systematic theology? What if its goal is simply to perform the indispensable task of trying to deal consistently, honestly, and systematically with the major theological issues of history as seen from the perspective of a man fully immersed in his own epoch? It need not then seek to create a school or attempt to provide a platform on which all knowledge must rest.

Tillich stated that "a system should be not only a point of arrival but a point of departure as well. It should be like a station at which preliminary truth is crystallized on the endless road toward truth." From this point of view, Paul Tillich's systematic theology and his theological approach meet the most rigorous tests of contemporary relevance and possible survival. Tillich sketched out the basic issues that are now and will remain for a long time to come the fundamental questions confronting Christian theology in the modern world. He ventured answers which will continue to be a key station or point of departure on the endless road toward truth. His theology will be one of the basic points of contact in the rapidly developing Roman Catholic–Protestant dialogue.

Above all, Paul Tillich made it possible for countless modern men to become or remain Christian without ceasing to be modern men. He demonstrated what it meant to love God with the mind as well as with the heart and the soul. He affirmed the doubts and insecurities of modern man, for he shared these fully, and only in this way could he point beyond them to the ground of hope. His life and his theology were a unity in joyfully embracing the world. He was charmed, fascinated, and awed by the very fact of this universe and the people in it. He participated fully in its suffering and frustration, yet he never ceased to extol its goodness grounded in the Creator. It was because Paul Tillich lived so fully in the world and loved it so deeply that he constantly pointed beyond it—to the depth of its reality, to the richness of the eternal which alone makes it meaningful.

His theology remains a paradigm for the way a truly modern man can be a God-possessed man—to be rooted in the ground of being and so to stand in the midst of the world, appreciatively, sensitively, sorrowing, suffering, enjoying, rejoicing, and loving. Such a view cannot be based on an episodic or *ad hoc* theology. One cannot live long on the boundary on a purely pragmatic basis. The longer Americans live on the boundary, the more they will realize this and learn there is no easy answer, not even the Christian faith. Perhaps this is Paul Tillich's greatest legacy to modern man. He exemplified in life and thought how to affirm faith through doubt.

His own words expressed this most eloquently.

"But if we accept the message of the new reality in the Christ, we must understand that this message does not contain an easy answer, and that it does not guarantee any spiritual security. We must know that it is a real answer only if we understand it permanently in the light of our human situation, in which tragedy and hope fight each other without victory. The victory is above them. The victory came when the prayer of the psalmist was answered. 'Relent, O thou Eternal'—this prayer is the prayer of mankind though all eons, and is the hidden prayer in the depth of every human soul."[1]

[1] Paul Tillich, *The Shaking of the Foundations* (New York: Charles Scribner's Sons, 1948), p. 75.

~~~~~ *The Sources*

of Paul Tillich's Richness – WILHELM PAUCK

EVERYONE among us who has known, respected, or loved Paul
Tillich has sensed that he was endowed with extraordinary gifts,
and that he was a man of great spiritual and intellectual riches.
As we mourn his death, we can say that, because of his gifts, he
fulfilled himself.

He embodied in his person a marvelously varied heritage which
he deepened and expanded throughout the years of his long life.
Paul Tillich was a truly cultivated man, and as such a humanist
as well as a humanitarian. He knew that the dignity of man rests
on the willingness and ability of the individual to appropriate for
himself the legacy of his fathers and forefathers, to evaluate and
to judge this legacy in relation to himself and his own times, then
to mould it, if need be, by giving it new forms, and finally to hand
it on to his own heirs.

In all his works and throughout his activities, Paul Tillich gave
expression to this dimension of life in which man is most authen-
tically human. One can say, I believe, that he exercised the responsibility for a creative reception of his own legacy in a highly
personal way. He was acutely aware of his indebtedness to his
parents, especially his father, and he remembered in very poignant
ways what he owed to his teachers. Moreover, throughout his life,
he expressed gratitude to the friends of his youth for what they
had given to him, and in his mind he carried vivid memories of
the times and circumstances when he had learned something new.

23

His thinking was autobiographical in a remarkable way. That is why, in the introduction to his books, he tended to interpret his subjects by references to the way in which they had become important to him in his own development. Thus his readers came to know him more personally than authors are generally known to their audience. The same can be said about the effect of his lectures because he made his hearers feel how he himself had become involved in what he was speaking to them about, and he liked to refer to the decisive encounters or occasions which had aroused or stimulated new turns in his thinking.

To give some examples: he often alluded to his early years in the small towns of Starzeddel and Schönfliess in Prussia where his father was an Evangelical minister and where he grew up. He then made one understand why he loved old customs and usages as they are preserved in the communities of small towns and villages. At the same time, he made one feel why he was so deeply attached to evangelical-Lutheran piety. As a child, he had absorbed it in his father's house, and he held on to it throughout his life, even though he came to transcend it in the context of his mature theology. He always remained a Protestant of the Evangelical Church of Prussia. One who knows the ways and customs of this part of Christianity could feel that Paul Tillich derived his pristine sense for religion from there and could understand how he remained at home in this tradition as a theologian as well as a preacher. In his later years, he was not at all interested in churchmanship or denominationalism, but he always relied on the legacy of the church of his father.

In a similar way, he never failed to let his readers and hearers know what he owed to the classical training of the German *Gymnasium* and university and what specifically he had received from certain teachers. In theology, he felt most indebted to Martin Kähler, a professor of systematic theology at the University of Halle; and, in philosophy, to Fritz Medicus, then also a teacher at Halle. Kähler, who must have been a powerful person who effectively communicated his ideas to his students, gave Tillich the insight that even our thinking is broken and is in need of justification and that therefore any dogmatism of thought is the intellectual form of Pharisaism. Loyalty to Kähler prevented Paul Tillich from being a dogmatist. Medicus introduced him to the German Idealists and particularly to Schelling and thus determined the course and basic character of his entire philosophical thought. Of this he was always conscious.

I remember that he once told me that when he was ready to read the works of Schelling, he so concentrated on them that he forced himself to exclude all wanderings from his mind in order to be able to re-think Schelling's ideas and to make sense of them. No wonder that echoes of the thought of Schelling resound throughout Tillich's philosophical theology, yet not by way of a slavishly exact reproduction; they have become transformed by being put in new relations.

In a similar way, Paul Tillich dealt with the rich legacy of the thinkers whose methods or ideas he adopted for himself. He knew them thoroughly; having thought through what he read of them, he freely made them his own. This is the reason why he was not a scholar in the strict sense of the word but rather a wise man, not a man of learning but rather an intuitive, creative thinker.

As a teacher and writer, he was first of all an interpreter of theology who addressed himself to the contemporary religious situation—but what a wealth of historical thought he brought to bear on his endeavor to render theological ideas and doctrines meaningful for today! Somehow the thinkers with whom he felt a kinship were always present in his thought—the pre-Socratics and particularly Parmenides with his question, "Why is there not nothing?"; Plato and Plotinus and their teaching on essences; the Stoics and their doctrine of the Logos; Augustine with his complex doctrine of God as infinite truth which can be immediately experienced in the depth of the soul, and as infinite will which nobody can ever fully comprehend; Eckhart, Cusanus, and particularly Luther with his teaching on the God of wrath and love; and Boehme with his brooding on God, the ground and abyss of being; and then finally the great German thinkers—Kant, Schelling, Hegel, and Schleiermacher. Beginning with them, Tillich again and again coursed through the history of Western thought, backward to the early Greeks and forward to the present day, deeply stirred up and stimulated by the impetus he had received from the thought of the thinkers who had revolutionized the modern intellectual world—Kierkegaard, Nietzsche, Marx, and Freud.

II

In connection with all this we must next consider what it meant for Tillich that his career took its course through three distinct periods of Western history and that he experienced them by participating deeply in them as a passionately responsible contemporary.

He grew up and reached manhood during the last and mature phase of the civilization of the nineteenth century when men, especially men of Germany, content with the fact that they had succeeded in maintaining peace in the world for several decades, were confident that this would remain so, possibly forever, and therefore circled around their own self-sufficiency.

Then he experienced the collapse of this world in the First World War, during which he served as a chaplain in the German army.

As he commenced his career as a university-teacher (in 1919, in Berlin), all he had absorbed of the cultural life had, he felt, a break in it. The German nation, Western civilization, mankind had to be renewed and healed. Tillich was resolved to help bring about this renewal. He became one of those Germans who believed that the downfall of the militaristic-national monarchies of Europe and the rise of socialist democracies set the stage for a general cultural reformation in accordance with the vision of a new humanism that was intended to be true to the requirements of modern life, as well as to the inherited ideals of Jewish, Greek, and Christian origins.

Holding successive professorships at Marburg, Dresden, and Frankfurt, he was at the same time a prominent leader of the Religious Socialists. They hoped to save the socialist parties from falling victim to utopianism by suffusing their outlook with the teachings of what Tillich called "belief-ful realism." They also hoped to save the Christian churches from becoming socially and politically irrelevant by causing them to concern themselves constructively with the problems of modern technological-industrial society.

Hitler and the Nazis put an end to all this. Paul Tillich was dismissed from his professorship. The hopes he had cherished were dashed; what he had come to fear with increasing clarity had come to pass.

Powerless and impoverished he emigrated to this country. Union Theological Seminary gave him the chance to rebuild his career. While he struggled to learn the English language and became acquainted with the ways of American academic institutions, he joined the Fellowship of Socialist Christians led by Reinhold Niebuhr and thus was initiated into a characteristically American form of social criticism and activism, just at the time when the New Deal program of Franklin D. Roosevelt took shape. He also assumed the chairmanship of the organization known as "Self-Help" which assisted German refugees in their attempt to get a foothold and fresh start in this country. Thus his interests continued to be concentrated on political developments and, within his own circles, he remained in politics.

During the Second World War he hoped that, once victory over Hitler was achieved, a constructive peace settlement would be made within the establishment of a United Europe supported by an international union of the nations of the world. When it became clear that these aims could not be attained, Paul Tillich resignedly proclaimed the doctrine of "the sacred void," which means that as long as it proves impossible to formulate and execute a realistic program for world reconstruction, men must wait responsibly for the right moment, ready to take advantage of the opportunities of the *kairos* when it comes.

Without giving up his keen interest in political and social affairs, he then turned to the task of writing his *Systematic Theology* which he had first projected in Marburg in 1925. He lectured on it throughout the following years. When it was finally completed in 1963, it was recognized everywhere as a constructive work of greatest importance. This systematic theology is utterly different from similar works because it bears the marks of having been written by one who, on passing with utmost consciousness through great historical changes, had never ceased to think of plans of action for himself and his fellowmen through which a true humanity would be realized, namely a way of life which renders man human and separates him from all that is inhuman, superhuman, or subhuman. Hence he could write about his work as a Protestant theologian, as follows:

I have tried to look at Protestantism from the outside as well as the inside. From the outside: first from the point of view of a passionately loved and studied philosophy, and, in later years, from the point of view of a powerfully developing history of religion; and, finally, from the point of view of the experienced and interpreted general history of our period.[1]

III

All this shows that Paul Tillich had a clear sense of vocation. He felt himself called to be a teacher of men who, having come to know their questions, helped them to find answers. He fulfilled this calling with an intense consciousness. He was always awake to all the possibilities of any occasion and eager to comprehend the meaning contained in these possibilities. This is why he was such an extraordinarily effective teacher. Despite the fact that he used

[1] Paul Tillich, *The Protestant Era* (Chicago, 1948), p. 11.

hardly any oratorical or rhetorical tricks (for he always spoke in a quiet, even tone of voice), he deeply aroused his hearers, giving them the sure feeling that he understood them and their basic questions and that he could speak to them helpfully. Yet he never gave easy answers.

"My whole theological work," he said only recently, "has been directed to the interpretation of religious symbols in such a way that the secular man—and we are all secular—can understand and be moved by them."[2] In order to accomplish this end he had trained himself to think of each problem in the fullest possible context, and at the same time with the greatest possible clarity. He combined the art of dialectical, with that of systematic thinking, seeking for truth by talking with others from different points of view, moving through Yes and No, and then proceeding to put the results of such thinking together in an orderly system of thought. He was at the same time a sharp, critical analyst and a highly skillful, constructive thinker.

Many people found his thought difficult and some even turned away from him because they felt that his ideas were too involved, or too abstract. But he was certain he was living up to his calling. He regarded the intellect as a God-given function which had to be used to the fullest extent. To think about the structure of reality was, he firmly believed, the theologian's job. He adhered to the discipline which this required from the beginning of his career to its end. Throughout his life, he produced ideas which startled those who received them because they were so illuminating or suggestive or helpful.

IV

One final remark about the richness of Paul Tillich's personality: At all times he was willing to share what he possessed. Though he kept and guarded the secret of his own personality for himself,

[2] Paul Tillich, *Ultimate Concern*, ed. by D. M. Brown (New York: Harper & Row, 1965), p. 88.

his mind was wonderfully open to the concerns of others and he liberally gave to them of the treasures of his own life. This is why his death now leaves a void in the lives of many all over the world.

He loved to be with and among people and to discuss with them almost any question that happened to be brought up. Throughout his life, from the days of his youth until the years of his old age, he learned more from conversations, discussions and debates than from books, although having said this, I must hasten to add that he diligently and industriously read many books.

In a letter to Thomas Mann, written on May 23, 1943, in which he reviewed his student years, he wrote,

"The summer semester of 1907, when I was the presiding officer of the student-corporation 'Wingolf' numbering then about seventy men, appears to me until today as the greatest period of my life. What I have become as a theologian, a philosopher, a man, I owe partly to my professors but mostly to this fraternity. The theological and philosophical debates we had then till late after midnight and the personal conversations before dawn, have remained decisive for my entire life."

This is a confession which is very characteristic of Paul Tillich. He was always a mediator and a bridge-builder, living and working in the midst of men, at all times surrounded by a cloud of witnesses with each of whom he would, sooner or later, be personally in touch.

Because this was his way he became, and was, so rich.

Paul Tillich and the

History of Religions – MIRCEA ELIADE

IT IS significant, and it is perhaps symbolic, that the last public lecture of Paul Tillich was entitled "The Significance of the History of Religions for the Systematic Theologian." In the course of that superb and moving lecture, Professor Tillich declared that, had he time, he would write a new *Systematic Theology* oriented toward, and in dialogue with, the whole history of religions. In his *Systematic Theology* Tillich had addressed himself to modern Western men, at grips with history and totally involved in the secular world of science and technology. He felt now that a new systematic theology was needed—a theology taking into consideration not only the existential crisis and the religious vacuum of contemporary Western societies, but also the religious traditions of Asia and the primitive world, together with their recent crises and traumatic transformations.

As a matter of fact, Paul Tillich had been attracted to History of Religions since his student years. He loved the Greek language and mythology as much as he loved Greek philosophy; he followed the works of Rudolph Otto, C. G. Jung, and Arnold Toynbee with great interest; and he wrote about religious symbolism repeatedly and with a unique acumen. But it seems to me that his old interest in History of Religions was reawakened and increased by his voyage to Japan and his encounter with Buddhist and Shinto priests and scholars. The impact of this visit on Tillich's entire life and thought was tremendous. For the first time he had

31

immersed himself in a living and extremely varied religious milieu which was completely different from that of the Mediterranean and Judeo-Christian traditions. He was equally impressed and moved by the Shintoist, cosmic type of religion and by the Buddhist and Zen schools.

This profound experience, simultaneously religious and cultural, was only partially expressed in his Bampton lectures, *Christianity and the Encounter of the World Religions*, delivered at Columbia University in 1961 and published in book form two years later. Eager to analyze the origins and structure of what he called quasi-religions—i.e. liberal humanism, fascism and communism—Paul Tillich did not have time enough to elaborate his conception of a meaningful dialogue between drastically different religions. But he made it clear that one should not initiate an inter-religious discussion "with a comparison of the contrasting concepts of God or man or history or salvation," but with a more radical question, namely "the question of the intrinsic aim of existence—in Greek, the *telos* of all existing things." And, on the basis of his own recent experiences in Japan, he consecrated one of his lectures to the Christian–Buddhist dialogue, proceeding from this very central question: the intrinsic aim or *telos* of existence. With his powerful and systematic mind, he presented in this way what he called the two *telos*-formulas—"in Christianity, the *telos* of every*one* and everything united in the Kingdom of God; in Buddhism the *telos* of every*thing* and everyone fulfilled in Nirvana."

The entire chapter abounds in such illuminating formulas and revelatory insights. But this little book signifies only the beginning of a new phase in Paul Tillich's thought. We came to understand how deeply he was attracted by the non-Christian religions when he proposed a joint seminar on History of Religions and Systematic Theology. Those evening meetings in the winter and autumn quarters of 1964 constitute one of my most precious and lasting *souvenirs*. It was not just the amazing spectacle of a 78-year-old master being more alert and more resourceful, after three hours of discussion, than many members of the seminar, including myself.

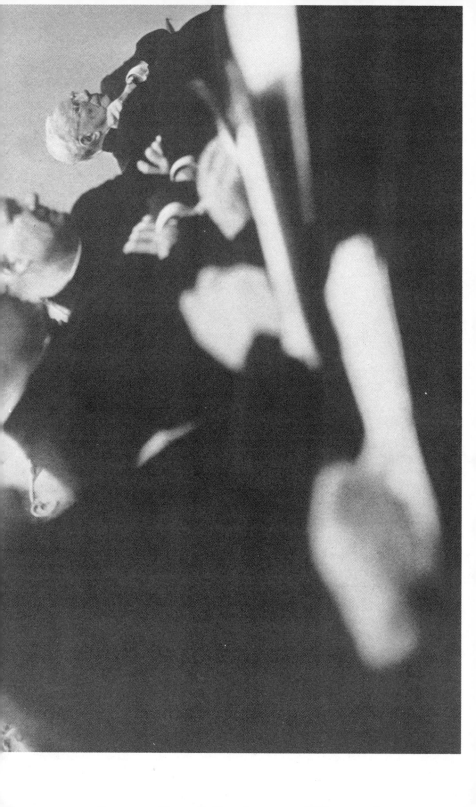

With Cardinal Suenens

Dialogue Conference

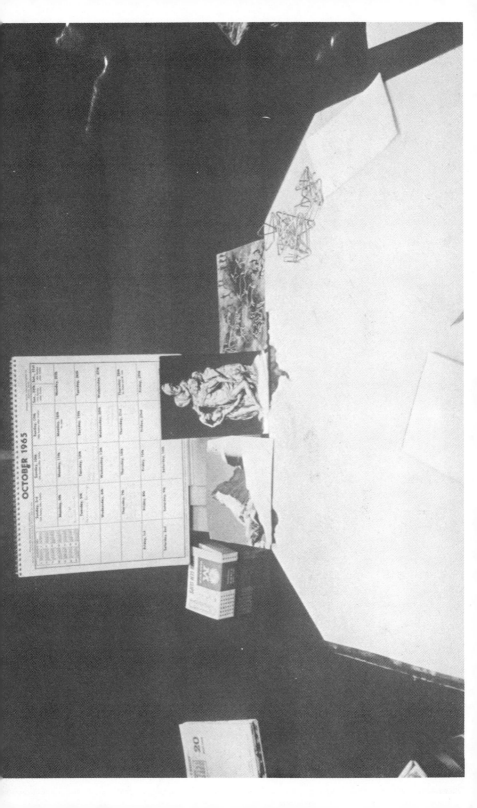

It was the almost charismatic experience of witnessing a creative mind in the very process of creation. Of course, we all knew his astonishing powers of systematization—and it was refreshing to see how the immense and heteroclite materials brought forward by the historians of religion would disclose their structures and by this very fact become susceptible of classification and analysis. But the unique experience was following Tillich's mind as it confronted the unfamiliar, archaic or oriental, religious fact—a cosmogonic myth, an initiation ritual, an eccentric divine figure, a strange but religious form of behavior, and so on. He was always able to grasp not only the religious meaning of such a fact, but also its human value. For him it revealed a specific—even if in some cases a rather aberrant—encounter with the sacred. And perhaps just because he was a daring theologian, unafraid of meeting the secular world on its own ground, he could have also become a very original and sensitive historian of religions, for he was not afraid of the strangeness and sometimes almost demonic expressions of religious experience.

But, of course, Paul Tillich would never have become a historian of religions nor, as a matter of fact, a *historian* of anything else. He was interested in the existential meaning of history—*Geschichte*, not *Historie*. When confronted with archaic, traditional, and oriental religions, he was interested in their historical concreteness and immediacy, not in their modifications or changes or in the results of the flowing of time. He did not deny the importance of the temporal flux for the understanding of the history of specific religious forms—but he was primarily interested in their structures; he deciphered their meaning in grasping their structures.

At a certain moment during our joint seminar, I thought that Paul Tillich was in the process of elaborating a theology of History of Religions. But very soon I realized that his mind was working in another direction. What he was accomplishing in our unforgettable evenings was a *renewal of his own Systematic Theology*. Now, every student of Paul Tillich's works knows very well that one of the dominant characteristics of his thought was a capacity for renewing itself after an encounter with a radically different, and even inimical, ideology or historical situation. Such was the case during the First World War, when he immersed himself in Nietzsche's philosophy and discovered, as Nietzsche had already prophetically proclaimed, that the God of the German and European bourgeoisie was dead. Through Nietzsche and through the terrors of the war, Tillich became aware of the importance of history for modern man; thus he accepted his responsibilities and became one of the outstanding members of the German Christian–Socialist party. Paul Tillich's creative thinking was stirred by this confrontation with his historical moment. But although he recognized the urgency of social and political reforms, he became neither a political leader nor a socialist philosopher. He saw himself as a religious man, a Christian and a philosopher, and he struggled to discover what new understanding of Christianity might permit one to call himself Christian while living at the same time in the historical world. Later in his life Paul Tillich was to take more and more seriously the scientific and technological progress which so drastically transformed the modern western world. Some of his most important books, and particularly his *Systematic Theology*, were written for the believers who survived in a society rapidly being secularized—but also for the nonbelievers—trying to show them what it means to be a religious man, and specifically a Christian, in a world without God.

Thus the creative life of Paul Tillich was marked by a series of encounters with non-Christian and non-religious realities which he simply could not ignore, for they were part and parcel of his historical moment and, as a genuine Christian existentialist, he could not turn his back to history. But what must be pointed out is the continual renewal of Tillich's thought as a result of the challenges which he recognized in Nietzsche's proclamation of the death of God, in the horrors of the war, in the social and political struggles, and in the triumph of science and technology.

34

Now it seems to me that a similar creative process had started after Paul Tillich's encounter with archaic and oriental religions. We witnessed in our seminars how Tillich was fighting his way to a new understanding of systematic theology. The importance of this creative activity was not simply that it was something *new*, but that it was significant, and it will be even more so in the near future. Many times in the past the creative thinking of Paul Tillich anticipated what were later on to become rather popular movements and ideologies. He was an existentialist and wrote on the meaning of history long before existentialism became fashionable and history became a cliché. And, as he recognized in the preface to the third volume of his *Systematic Theology*, his conceptions of nature and life are very close to the ideas of Teilhard de Chardin—although he did not discover the books of this author until after he had finished his work. As is well known, Teilhard de Chardin's tremendous success is due in great part to his religious valorization of matter and life. Tillich's theological meditations on the same subject denote not only a structural similarity between these two great minds, but also how correctly they anticipated the central problematic of the new generation of believers and nonbelievers. And, exactly as in the case of Teilhard de Chardin, it is probable that Tillich's influence will prove to be more powerful and stimulating after his death.

We will never know what would have been the result of Paul Tillich's encounter with primitive and oriental religions. But it is highly significant that he surmised the decisive role of such confrontations, not only for the Christian theologian, but also for the world at large. Indeed, we are already approaching a planetary culture, and before long even the most provincial historian, philosopher or theologian will be compelled to think through his problems and formulate his beliefs in dialogue with colleagues from other continents and believers in other religions.

Thus, in his last discoveries and his last theological preoccupations, Paul Tillich was again an innovator and a precursor. Faithful to his vocation and his destiny, Paul Tillich did not die at the end of his career, when he had supposedly said everything important that he could say. On the contrary, he died at the beginning of another renewal of his thought. Thus his death is even more tragic, for theologian and historian of religion alike. But it is also symbolic.

Essays by Paul Tillich

The Effects of Space
Exploration on Man's Condition and Stature

THE subject under discussion has two sides; the one is the effect of space exploration on man as such, and the other is its effect on man's view of himself; the first requires more a report about man's condition, the second more a valuation of man's stature in consequence of the space exploration. But this distinction cannot be maintained when one goes into the concrete problems which have arisen as an effect of space research and space travel. A decisive part of man's condition, as it is caused by his penetration into space beyond the gravitation of the earth, is his self-evaluation on the basis of this achievement. On the other hand, its conflicting evaluations are brought out by the contrast of the negative and positive effects of space exploration on the human condition. Therefore I intend to deal with the problems of our subject without any sharp demarcation between the effects of space exploration on the situation of man, and on his view of himself.

1. Historical Precedents

The present situation is the result of many steps made by Western man since the Renaissance. It would be unrealistic and would prevent an adequate answer if the last step, however important and unique it is, were considered in isolation from the previous steps. Many effects, both on man himself and his view of himself, appeared long ago; and it leads to a distortion of facts and valuations, if contemporaneous writers overemphasize the uniqueness of the present achievement in comparison with what has been done and thought before in the series of steps which have made the present one possible.

The Renaissance is not the rebirth of the ancient traditions as the term is often misunderstood, but it is the rebirth of Western society in all respects, religious, cultural and political with the help of the ancient sources of the Mediterranean civilization. In this process the traditions were transformed in many respects, due to the Christian background of the Renaissance. One of the most important transformations is the turn from the Greek contemplative and the medieval self-transcending ideals of life to the active, world-controlling and world-shaping ideal. This implied a high valuation of technical sciences and the beginning of that fertile interaction between pure and applied sciences which immensely contributed—and is still doing so—to the fast development of both of them. There was little of this interaction in Greece, the late ancient world and the Middle Ages; it was something new, not a repetition, but a rebirth. One may express the situation in three geometrical symbols, the circle for the fulfilment of life within the cosmos and its potentialities—as found in classic Greece; the vertical or the striving of life toward what transcends the cosmos, namely the transcendent One, the ultimate in being and meaning—as found in late antiquity and in the Middle Ages; the horizontal or the trend toward the control and transformation of the cosmos in the service of God or man—as found in the period since the Renaissance, Reformation and Enlightenment. The "discovery of the horizontal" is the first step in a development in which space exploration is the preliminary last step. Both are victories of the horizontal over the circular and the vertical line.

The transition from the vertical to the horizontal line in the determination of the "telos," the inner aim of human existence, was greatly helped by the astronomy of the Renaissance and the related "utopian" literature. The Copernican astronomy had thrown the earth out of the center of the universe—the least divine of all places—and elevated it to the dignity of a star amongst other stars. About the same time a highly influential philosopher, Nicholas of Cusa, taught the immanence of the infinite within the finite, e.g. in earth and man. This raised the significance of everything in the world by making it an expression of the divine life and it gave impetus to the expectations of a fulfilment of history on this planet. The "utopian" literature shows visions of a future which unites religious, political, economic and technical elements. This again raised the importance of technology in relation to the pure sciences far above what it was in Greece and the intermediary periods. Typical for this situation is Leonardo da Vinci who combined the anticipation of the ideal in his paintings with empirical studies of natural phenomena and with technical experiments—in which, just as today, techniques of war played a great role.

In the seventeenth century the realization of the problems, implied in these beginnings of the modern period of Western history, increased and found a characteristic expression in Pascal's confrontation of man's smallness with his greatness. He experienced with many of his contemporaries the shock of man's smallness in view of the universe of recent astronomy. At the same time, he experienced in his own work as mathematician and physicist the power of the human mind to penetrate into the calculable structures of nature, his greatness even in face of the quantitative vastness of the universe. In Pascal many problems of man's present self-interpretation are anticipated. The human predicament in its contradictory character is shown just as we see it today. And he also asked the question which is highly relevant for our problem: What has become, under the control of the horizontal line, of the vertical one, the line toward what transcends the cosmos? He answered with his famous words which contrast the "God of Abraham, Isaac and Jacob" with the "god of the philosophers." He himself was struggling to save the dimension of the ultimate, which transcends the greatness as well as the smallness of man. He did it for himself, but the development followed the horizontal line in the eighteenth century belief in human progress; in the nineteenth cenutry belief in universal evolution; in the ideologies supporting the industrial, social and political revolutions of the three last centuries. There were always theological, mystical, romanticist and classicist attempts to recover the vertical line or to return to the circular world view of classical Greece. But the drive towards that which lies ahead proved to be stronger than the longing back to a world in which it is more important to look at the eternal essences of the cosmos than to anticipate a future to be created by man.

One of the shocks connected with the removal of man and his earth from the cosmic center was basically theological. Since the Biblical literature as well as its interpretation in fifteen hundred years of church history was based on a world view in which the earth was in the center of the universe, and human history the ultimate aim of the creation of the earth, and the Christ the center of human history—an urgent question arose: What about the position of man in the providential acting of God, what about the cosmic significance of the Christ in the universe as a whole? Does not the moving of the earth out of the center undercut both the central significance of man and the cosmic significance of the Christ? Is not the whole "drama of salvation" reduced to a series of events, happening on a small planet at a particular time without universal significance?

With these problems, already alive in the Western world, the age of space exploration started.

II. The Emotional Reaction to Space Exploration

The first reaction to the break through the gravitational field of the earth was naturally astonishment, admiration, pride, increased by the national pride of those who achieved the breakthrough, diminished but not annihilated by the feeling of national humiliation of those who could have achieved it but did not. Yet there was almost no exception to a feeling of astonishment about man's potentialities, hidden up to then, but now revealed: Man is not only able to explore transterrestrial space, he is also able to change the astronomical picture by adding something to what was given to him by nature. Admiration was particularly directed to the theoretical and technical intelligence of those who were responsible for the successful penetration of the earthly sphere, and to the moral courage of those who risked their life in actualizing what was a human potentiality and had now become real. A consequence of this admiration was the status of heroic pioneers, given to the astronauts, even to those in the enemy camp, and of bearers of esoteric wisdom, unattainable for most human beings, given to the atomic scientists. The emotional power of these reactions is very strong and not without important sociological effects. They became symbols, and thus decisive for the formation of a new ideal of human existence. The image of the man who looks down at the earth, not from heaven, but from a cosmic sphere above the earth became an object of identification and psychological elevation to innumerable people.

The same image unlocked streams of imagination about encounters inside and outside the gravitational field of the earth with non-earthly, though not heavenly (or hellish) beings. The largeness of the literature of scientific fiction, often done as a sideline by scientists themselves, preceded as well as followed the actual progress of space exploration. But it reached its full extension only after actual achievements in this direction had been attained. Its real importance is not the occasional anticipation of scientific or technical discoveries, but it is the fulfilment of the desire of man to transcend the realm of earth-bound experiences, at least in imagination. The so-called "Gothic" novel did this with the help of supranatural divine and demonic interferences in the natural processes of life, the spiritualistic novel did it through the ambiguity of psychic phenomena which appeared as neither unambiguously natural nor unambiguously supranatural. Science-fiction, especially if connected with space exploration, transcends the bondage to the earth by imagining encounters with natural but transterrestrial beings. Mythological as well as psychic supranaturalism are replaced by a transterrestrial naturalism: the earth is transcended, not through something qualitatively other, but through a strange section of something qualitatively the same—the natural universe.

At this point an observation can be made which should have some restraining effect on the drive toward earth-transcending imaginations (whether they are called experiences or mere phantasy): the content of these imaginations is always a combination of elements taken from earthly experience. The "beings" whose pictures are given are either glorified (angels and heavenly saints), or vilified duplications of the human figure (demons and inmates of hell), or they are combinations of elements by which the human figure is disfigured, as in scientific fiction. This shows a definitive limit on man's possibility of escaping the bondage to his earth even in imagination. The imagined worlds are construed with parts or elements of earthly experiences, even if these experiences are religious or artistic.

The last remark leads to another basically negative group of emotional reactions to space exploration. It has somehow concretely raised man's awareness of the immensity of the universe and the spatial distances in it. Just the experience of bridging some of these distances and consequently imagining the bridging of more of them have increased the sensitivity to the actual remoteness of even the nearest solar system beyond our own. The dizziness felt by people at Pascal's time facing the empty spaces between the stars has been increased in a period in which man has pushed not only cognitively but also bodily into these spaces. His anxiety of lostness in a small corner of the universe, which has balanced pride in his controlling power since the time of the eighth Psalm, has grown with the growth of the controlling power. One of the reasons for this anxiety is the loss of the ultimate transcendent above the greatness and the smallness of man—the answer to the question of man's predicament by the Psalm as well as by Pascal. The other, more particular reason, unknown to both of them, is the fact that man can use his controlling power for self-destruction, not only of parts of mankind, but of all of it. The intimate relation of space exploration to preparation for war has thrown a deep shadow over the emotionally positive reaction to space exploration. And this shadow will not recede as long as production of weapons and space exploration are tied up with each other.

III. Spiritual Consequences of Space Exploration

In describing the emotional effects of space exploration and its scientific precedents we have avoided value judgments except in an implicit way. It is, however, necessary to make them explicit and to discuss some ethical problems connected with our subject.

One of the results of the flight into space and the possibility of looking down at the earth is a kind of estrangement between man and earth, an "objectification" of the earth for man, the depriving "her" of her "motherly" character, her power of giving birth, of nourishing, of embracing, of keeping for herself, of calling back to herself. She becomes a large, material body to be looked at and considered as totally calculable. The process of demythologizing the earth which started with the early philosophers and was continued ever since in the Western world has been radicalized as never before. It is too early to realize fully the spiritual consequences of this step.

The same is true of another radicalization: the flight into transterrestrial space is the greatest triumph of the horizontal line over the vertical. We have gone forward in directions which are practically limitless while the farthest distances on earth are restricted to a half-circle which, if continued, leads in a full circle back to the beginning. However, this triumph of the horizontal raises serious spiritual problems, which all come down to the basic question: "For what?" Long before the break through the gravitational field of the earth the question "for what?" had been asked

with increasing seriousness and concern. It had been asked in connection with the endless production of means: machines, tools,
gadgets! It had been asked in connection with the question of the
meaning of life; and it had been asked, whenever the ways of
modern civilization in technology and business were subjected to
prophetic criticism, be it in religious or in secular terms. If the
question is now asked in connection with space exploration, it
becomes more abstract and more urgent than before. For here the
horizontal line is almost completely formalized. The aim is to go
forward for the sake of going forward, endlessly without a concrete focus. Of course, one could call the desire to learn more
about cosmic space and about astronomical bodies it in, a concrete
aim. But this is only an accidental aspect. The desire to go ahead
whatever may be encountered gives the real impetus. But just as
the *exclusive* surrender to the vertical line (in scepticism) leads
to the impossibility of expressing anything and acting in any direction, so also the *exclusive* surrender to the horizontal line (in
what one could call "forwardism") leads to the loss of any meaningful content and to complete emptiness. The symptoms of this
emptiness are already conspicuously among us in the form of
indifference, cynicism and despair. And space exploration is not
the means of healing it, but it may become a factor in deepening
it after the first enthusiasm has evaporated and the pride in man's
almost divine power (Ps. 8) has receded.

These spiritual dangers, however, should never lead to a decision to give up either the production of technical tools or
the attempts to penetrate into the outer-terrestrial spaces (as the
danger of radical mysticism should not lead to a rejection of the
mystical element in every religious experience). For danger is
not a reason to prevent life from actualizing its potentialities.

This leads to another problem, connected indirectly with our
subject, the problem of the responsibility of the scientist for dangerous possibilities implied in his discoveries. The problem is as
old as scholarly thought and was for millennia a source of conflict

between the priestly guardians of the holy and the prophetic or philosophical critics of the traditional beliefs. Even if the sociological, political and economic causes of such conflicts are taken into account, a genuine, tragic element remains: The priest is aware of the catastrophic consequences which criticism of holy traditions can have on the spirit of many people. But neither the prophet nor the philosopher can resign from his vocation to fight for justice and truth, even if sacred beliefs must be destroyed. This is probably the earliest example of the conflict between the safety of the given and the risk of the new. The dangers, connected with present scientific discoveries do not refer to the "salvation of souls" but to the very existence of mankind. But the problem itself and the tragic implications of any possible solution are the same. And the answer should be the same: Tragic consequences of the discovery and expression of truth are no reason for giving up the attempts to discover and the obligation to express truth. The danger for the soul of the believer should not keep the prophet or the Reformer from pronouncing truth in the vertical dimensions; and the danger of destructive consequences from scientific discoveries (including those in social sciences and psychology) should not keep the scientist from searching for and expressing truth in the horizontal dimension. It is bad to try to avoid tragedy if the price is to avoid truth. Therefore, even if space exploration, through its military implications, increases the chances of tragedy, this would not be a reason for stopping it. But such danger would be a powerful motive to balance the horizontal by the vertical line, to receive weapons against ultimate tragedy. In other words: The answer to the tragic implication of the pursuit of the horizontal line is not to break off this pursuit but to continue it under the criteria coming from the vertical line. But, one asks, is this still a possibility? Has not the power of the horizontal drive, especially in its scientific expressions almost cut off the relation to what transcends the universe and its scientific exploration? Has not man's image of himself in all Western religions been made obsolete by the horizontal dynamics of the last five hundred years? And does not space exploration pronounce the last word in this respect?

There is no doubt that science has undercut the cosmic frame within which man has seen himself in Biblical literature and ecclesiastical teaching, namely as the bearer of the history of salvation for the universe, as the *only* creature in whose nature God could become fully manifest, as he who will experience his own historical end as the end of the universe. Today's astronomy considers the possibility of other religiously meaningful histories in other parts of the universe, with other beings in whom God could have become fully manifest for them, with another beginning and another end, equally separated by a gap of uncounted billions of years as human history is from the beginning and the end of the universe (if such categories can be applied here at all). If space exploration is seen in this context, as the preliminary last step in a long development, one can say that it has changed tremendously the cosmic frame of man's religious self-evaluation. But one must add that it has not changed the divine-human relationship which had been experienced and symbolically expressed within this frame. Therefore one can answer the question, whether the dynamics of the horizontal have cut off the vertical, with a definite No! It is still possible for man to transcend tragedy and break through the horizontal movement with its tragic implications for the vertical and with its power to restrict. This "stature and condition" of man has not changed, although the way of its actualization must be different from that of periods in which the horizontal line had not yet shown its driving power.

IV. Sociological Consequences of Space Exploration

While the question of the right of scientific inquiry to go ahead without considering possibly dangerous consequences was answered affirmatively, another question arises to which an answer must be given. It is the economic question, how much of the income of a nation (or of all nations) should be given to space exploration? A main argument against space exploration is the immense amount of money needed for it which, according to the critics, should be used for more important projects, e.g. cancer-research or study of the best ways of restricting the increase of the world population. In both cases it is the conquest of bodily evils, disease and hunger, to which priority is given. This seems to be natural from the point of view of justice and agape. But actually it is neither natural nor was it ever real. Agape requires that the individual be always ready to help the sick and the poor in personal encounters as well as in social projects. And justice demands of society and its political representatives the continuous fight against the structures of evil in all its forms. But neither justice nor agape prohibits the use of economic power for cultural production. Otherwise no human potentiality, neither scientific nor technical, neither artistic nor ritual, neither educational nor social could ever have been actualized. But they *have* been actualized at a tremendous cost, and in their development they have produced powerful weapons against the structures of evil (mostly without intending to do so).

"Priority of needs" cannot mean that the whole cultural process should not have been started before the most immediate needs, e.g. conquering hunger and disease, had been satisfied. The term "priority" in the context of our problem is meaningful only in a particular situation. The question is: Which demand on the economic reserves of any social group has priority in this moment? And if a definite preference is established, the next question is: In which proportion shall economic aid be given to the preferred project in relation to other important projects? Finally it must be considered whether the rejection of one project, e.g. the next phase of space exploration, implies the certainty, or even a real chance, that one of the alternative projects will be accepted by the responsible authorities. It is, for example, highly improbable that the money saved by the stopping of space exploration would become available for cancer research or a restriction

49

of the population explosion. Beyond this, all these considerations would become academic in the moment in which it is manifest that space exploration has military consequences and belongs to the realm of competition with a potential enemy. Then it has priority over against all projects without direct military importance. The decision lies in the hands of those who have knowledge of the relevant factors and the power to balance the different points of view in terms of priorities and on the basis of the actual situation. They cannot be bound by a static hierarchy of priorities. Their only criterion should be the human aim of all political decisions (which certainly transcends national power as well as scientific progress). In this they are subject to the judgment of their conscience, the criticism of their contemporaries and the later judgment of history.

But here a conflict arises which is intensified by the sociological implications of space exploration: It contributes greatly to a general trend in our period, the growth of esoteric groups who through their knowledge and their inventiveness by far surpass what can be reached even by highly learned and productive people, not to speak of the vast majority of human beings. Such elites are esoteric and exclusive, partly through natural selection, partly through public prestige, partly through skillful exercise of their power. An aristocracy of intelligence and will to power has developed in the West as well as in the East and equalized to a considerable degree the two originally opposite social and political systems. Space exploration in the democratic world strengthens the antidemocratic elements, which are present in every democratic structure. There is a tendency in the average citizen, even if he has a high standing in his profession, to consider the decisions relating to the life of the society to which he belongs as a matter of fate on which he has no influence—like the Roman subjects all over the world in the period of the Roman empire, a mood, favorable for the resurgence of religion but unfavorable for the preservation of a living democracy.

It seems strange to raise the question of the consequences of space exploration for the ideal of education. But it is pertinent to the actual situation. If only the most extraordinary mathematical and technical intelligence can reach the top of the hierarchy of space theoreticians, and if only the most extraordinary bodily and psychological fitness can reach the top of the hierarchy of practical space explorers, it is understandable that these two types of man are raised to the place of ideal types according to which every individual should be formed, though in many degrees of approximation. This demand was made in this country most urgently after the success of the first Russian "Sputnik." There was a strong reaction on the part of the humanistically minded educators and also of many students who did not want or were not able to undergo the rigors of the education which would bring them to the top of the new hierarchy.

But the question is not solved by a transitory balance between the two ways of education or by the serious attempts to combine them. The preponderance of the non-humanistic way can hardly be overcome because of the actual structure of modern society and the impact it has on the life of every individual. It drives, often unconsciously, the most gifted and ambitious members of the younger generation into an educational system which guarantees them participation in the higher echelons of the social pyramid. Education cannot resist the solid structure of a social system and its demands on every individual in it. But again, this is no reason for cutting off space exploration or the developments on which it is based. For human nature is not expressed in its full potentialities by the horizontal line. Sooner or later it will revolt against the latter's predominance. And then space exploration will be judged in the light of the meaning of life in all its dimensions.

~~~~~~~~~~ *Frontiers*

FOR the high honor of this hour I can be grateful, I believe, to three border crossings made by the executive committee of the Marketing Union of the German Book Trade. They have crossed the national boundary and, as often before, awarded the Peace Prize to a citizen of another country. They have ignored the boundary between political action and spiritual work, and given the Peace Prize to someone who, if he has done anything at all, has served peace—that is, the realization of a universal human community—more through intellectual work than through political deed. And they have broken through the wall, strongly fortified by both sides, between culture and religion, and as a cultural organization bestowed the Peace Prize on a theologian. This three-fold border crossing is a very visible sign of the spirit in which the Peace Prize was established. My gratitude in this hour can only be an attempt to give by my words a philosophical and hence a religious and political expression to this spirit—for here, too, the boundaries are not final.

I would like to speak of "frontiers"—a concept which for long has awakened my philosophical as well as personal interests. "On the Boundary Line"/"Auf der Grenze" was the title I gave a small book of self-characterization with which I introduced myself in America shortly after emigration. And the little book which the *Evangelisches Verlagswerk* has brought out for today's celebration is entitled, "Auf der Grenze." The American book reported on many frontiers which are universally human and at the same time personal destiny: the boundary between country and city, between feudalism and civil service, between bourgeois society and Bohemianism, between church and society, between religion and culture, between theology and philosophy—and finally, on the personal side, between two continents.

Existence on the frontier, in the boundary situation, is full of tension and movement. It is in truth not standing still, but rather a crossing and return, a repetition of return and crossing, a back-and-forth—the aim of which is to create a third area beyond the bounded territories, an area where one can stand for a time without being enclosed in something tightly bounded. The frontier situation is not yet what one can call "peace"; and yet it is the portal through which every individual must pass, and through which the nations must pass, in order to achieve peace. For peace is to stand in the Comprehensive (*Übergreifenden*) which is sought in crossing and recrossing the frontiers. Only he who participates on both sides of a boundary line can serve the Comprehensive and thereby peace—not the one who feels secure in the voluntary calm of something tightly bounded. Peace appears where—in personal as well as in political life—an old boundary has lost its importance and thereby its power to occasion disturbance, even if it still continues as a partial boundary. Peace is not side-by-side existence without tension. It is unity within that which comprehends, where there is no lack of opposition of living forces and conflicts between the Old and the sometimes New—but in which they do not break out destructively, but are held in the peace of the Comprehensive.

If crossing and reversing the frontiers is the way to peace, then the root of disturbance and of war is the anxiety for that which lies on the other side, and the will to eliminate it which arises from it.

II

When destiny leads one to the frontier of his being, it makes him personally conscious that he stands before the decision either to fall back upon that which he already is or else to transcend himself. Every person is at that point led to the frontier of his being. He perceives the Other over beyond himself, and it appears to him as a possibility and awakens in him the anxiety of the potential. He sees in the mirror of the other his own limitedness, and he recoils; for at the same time this limitedness was his security, and now it is threatened. The anxiety of the potential draws him back into his bounded reality and its momentary calm. But the situation into which he will return is no longer the same. His experience of the potential and his failure toward it leaves a thorn behind, which cannot be eliminated, which can only be driven out of the consciousness by suppression. And where that occurs, there arises that spiritual phenomenon which we call fanaticism. The original meaning of the word is "divinely inspired." That is what the fanatic feels. But the word itself has changed its meaning, and one could rather say, "demoniacally inspired"—that is, born out of a distraught spiritual structure and thereby destructively fulfilled. That can appear in smaller, greater, or enormous measure, in persons and in groups.

I think of young students, theologians or perhaps natural scientists, who come to the universities from the security of tightly bounded thinking and belief; who are led there to the frontier of other thinking and belief; who realize what they themselves are like in the mirror of the other; who experience the potential but are not mature enough for it; who fall back on the old certainties, but now affirm them fanatically with the aim of eliminating the frontiers which they cannot cross over, of bringing all spiritual possibilities into subjection to their own, of dissolving them in their own identity. The aggression of the fanatic is the result of his weakness, his anxiety to cross over his own boundary, and his incapacity to see that realized in the other which he has suppressed in himself. It happens too that, in doubt toward his own spiritual world, one may cross the frontier, find in the new belief a new tightly bounded security, never go back again, and develop a counter-aggression—the often especially strong fanaticism of the renegade, the religious as well as the anti-religious. That is the ground out of which the wars of religion proceed. And if today they are no longer bloody wars, they are still battles that shatter the souls, in which the weapons of hate are used—namely, lies, distortion, exclusion, suppression—in order to eliminate the frontiers which one was too weak to cross over. Religious groups and whole churches can be driven into this posture. And it may be appropriate here to say a word about the German Protestant churches.

Perhaps before the church struggle there were groups among them who had indeed crossed the frontier, but who had not found their way back, and who exchanged the narrowness where they went—a critically emptied Christianity, for the narrowness from which they came—a traditionally calcified Christianity. Against the radically anti-Christian attacks of Nazism the churches had to draw back on the tradition and defend their identity at the cost of narrowing the boundary of their life. But their task today is to return to the frontier, to cross over it and wrestle for the Beyond in the to-and-fro between church and culture. If the churches do not risk this crossing of the frontier of their own identity, they will be irrelevant for unnumbered persons who, essentially, belong to them. And the thorn of having failed can produce a fanatical self-approval, which tries to incorporate culture into itself and remove the boundary against it.

Another example of the call to border–crossing may be given. It also begins with the individual and leads on to the situation of groups, here and now. I think of people who are confronted by the possibility of going out of their national or cultural boundaries, either for study or by personal encounters in one's own or a foreign land. For a moment the limits of their own cultural existence, their national or continental limitedness, are visible to them. But they cannot bear the sight. They cannot cross over the frontiers and seek for something Beyond.

The anxiety of the potential siezes them and drives them back. And the encounter with the stranger, which is a challenge to cross the frontier, becomes the occasion of a foreign-hating fanaticism.

The boundary which he is unable to cross over, man purposes to wipe out by destroying what is strange.

There is a social class among all industrial people which is admirably characterized by this conceptual framework: the lower middle class, the petit bourgeois, or—in a sociologically comprehensive symbol—the Philistine. Regardless of what social class he appears in, he can be exactly characterized as someone who—because of his anxiety at reaching his own frontier and seeing himself in the mirror of the different—can never risk rising above the habitual, the recognized, the established. He leaves unrealized the possibilities which are given every person from time to time to rise up out of himself—whether it is a person—who could have drawn him out of his narrowness, or an unusual work of art—which could have brought his security based on self into an upheaval. But all about him he sees people who have gone over the frontiers which he is unable to cross. And the secret envy becomes hate.

And, when in the Germany of the Hitler-period hate received unlimited power to fulfill itself, the frontiers were closed—so that a whole nation was unable to see beyond itself. And then the attempt was made to eliminate the frontiers by conquest or by destruction of that which lay on the other side of the boundary —whether they were other races or neighboring peoples, opposing political systems or new artistic styles, higher or lower social classes, or personalities developed through the crossing of borders. That is the demonic urge, perhaps in every person, to wipe out one's frontiers in order to be the whole thing by one's self.

Therefore I feel that I would not fulfill my task as a theologian did I not add a second point: first, that there are elements in all lands, and also in the United States, which correspond to the type of Philistine described. They raise their heads ever and again, not without success, but today in new forms and with numerous followers. And the second thing which I say only with trembling, as one for whom for years of his life Berlin was not only homeland but also a religious concept: everything which I have said about crossing the frontier is true too for crossing the line which is today hardest for the Western world to cross, the frontier toward the East. It is wrong when the Western peoples are prevented by education, literature and propaganda from crossing this frontier, which is erected not only in Berlin. We must also see what is going on in depth over there, and seek to understand it from a human standpoint—not just polemically. And I wish I were capable of saying that to those on the other side of the line, too.

The politically and spiritually responsible people of the West should fight for the point that the education of the peoples serves not only the inculcation and deepening of that which is their own, however great it may be, but that it lead out across the boundary —in knowledge, in understanding, in encounter, even if what is encountered seems to be only something standing in opposition. Encouragement to cross over from what is merely one's own— that is what education can contribute toward the achievement of peace. And more important than anything else at this point is education in a consciousness of history, which writes historical knowledge with historical understanding and is in no sense limited to class work in history.

III

Up to now we have spoken of crossing the frontier. But frontier is not only something to be crossed: it is also something which must be brought to fruition. Boundary is a dimension of form, and form makes everything what it is. The boundary between man and animal makes it possible to require and express things from men which can neither be required nor expected of an animal. The frontier between England and France made possible the development of two great—substantially different—cultures. The frontier between religion and philosophy makes possible the freedom of philosophical thought and the passion of religious submission. Definition is *ab-grenzung*, and without it there is no possibility of grasping or recognizing reality.

No culture was so aware of the significance of the boundary line as the Greeks. Plato and his Pythagorean predecessors attributed everything positive to the bounded and everything negative to the unbounded. Space, even self itself, is bounded. The figures of the gods, and the temple in which they are sculptured, remain measured by the standard of the human. Limiting thought must bound the passion which drives toward the unbounded. The tragic hero, who breaks out of the essential limit, is driven back by the gods—the protectors of frontiers—and destroyed. The essential limits of man are the subject of oracles and seers, tragedians and philosophers. They want to call back to them from the false, too narrow or too wide factual limits. For the essential limit and the factual limit do not coincide. The essential limit stands demanding, judging, giving goals beyond the factual limit.

In the younger generation, in the United States and outside as well, there has appeared a problem in recent years which is treated again and again in literature and discussion: "the search for identity." It is the expression of a period in which many are incapable of finding the essential limit in and beyond their passing factual limits, and not just alone as individuals, but also as members of society—national, cultural, religious. How can persons, how can peoples find their identity and thereby their true limits— when they lose their final meaning in the actual limits? That is the point where the question of the frontier and the question of peace merge with each other. For the one who has found his identity and thereby the frontier of his nature does not need to lock himself in or to break out. He will bring to fruition what his nature is. Of course, in that realization all the questions of the border crossings come back—but accompanied now by a consciousness of himself and his own potential. At all times and in all places mankind has undertaken something beyond its essential nature and its limits. The communicators of these insights, upon whom religious experiences, basic revelations as well as creative cultures depend, have expressed through laws and ordinances in various ways the essential limits for all that is human. They have given voice to the conscience of the individual, the voice of his essential nature, and they have shaped the ethos of the groups for long periods. But no life process is exhausted in the law alone. The essential nature also contains the goal, and words for frontier often also express the end toward which a life process strives— such as the Latin "finis," the Greek "telos."

For Socrates, the consciousness of this goal was the voice of his daemon, which showed to him his essential limit in difficult decisions. In Christianity it is the consciousness of being religiously guided—or, more dynamically, being driven by the Spirit. Among peoples it is the consciousness of calling, in which the identity— and with it the essential limit—of a nation expresses itself. The world–historical results of the consciousness of calling are extraordinary. They have been vastly decisive for the manner of peace and disturbance in the world of nations. The Greeks' consciousness of calling, to represent the humane against barbarism, saved Europe from the Persian invasion. Rome's consciousness of calling, to be the carrier of the idea of Law, created the unity of Mediterranean culture. Israel's consciousness of calling is the foundation for the three prophetic religions of the West. The German imperial consciousness of calling created the religio-political unity of the Middle Ages. The Italian consciousness of calling of the Renaissance courts achieved the renaissance of the Western world out of Roman and Christian antiquity, the French consciousness of calling—the civilization of the upper classes and the emancipation of the citizenry, the English consciousness of calling—the opening of the world in the spirit of Christian humanism, the Russian consciousness of calling before *and* after the Bolshevik revolution—hope for the salvation of the West from its individualistic corruption through a unity founded in religion or ideology. And the American consciousness of calling has created faith in a new beginning and the spirit of a crusade for its universal accomplishment. In all of these cases of consciousness of calling, a people found its essential limits and sought to make them into factual limits.

59

But thereby there occurred that which is responsible for the lack of peace and the tragedy of world history. The power which is necessary for every bringing to fruition of something alive has the tendency—in the political just as in the personal dimension—to cut loose from the goal which it should serve, that is, the realization of that calling, to become independent and then to develop a reality destructive of frontiers and contrary to nature. It is not power that is evil but the power which is cut loose from its essential limit. It is most violent when the consciousness of calling has lost its creative force, sometimes too, when the consciousness of calling is totally lacking.

And that seems to be the case with the Germany of the nineteenth and twentieth centuries. The failure of Germany, from the middle of the nineteenth century on, lay in the fact that it developed power without this power's being put at the service of a calling. What Bismarck called *Realpolitik* was power politics without a guiding consciousness of calling. And thereby Hitler could, with demoniacal ease, suggest the absurd racial consciousness of calling to broad circles of the German people—a facade, but an effective facade, for a development of power led by no true consciousness of calling.

Peace is possible where power stands in the service of a genuine consciousness of calling and knowledge of the essential limit, limits the importance of the factual limits. The fact that this foundation of politics was not admitted is the source of the German lack of peace in the twentieth century. The goal of all peaceful efforts in literature and politics should be that it be again accepted. Let peace speeches be avoided which, because they cannot help, do damage, since world history is so deeply rooted in the demonic. Pacifistic legalism demands the unconditioned holding fast to frontiers as they are in fact drawn today, here and now. It forgets the dynamics of world history and the creative and correcting effect of the essential frontier.

From this there is derived a second challenge to German political education, and finally to politics itself. The first was this: to lead to a crossing of the frontier, that is, the factual limit, and to conquer anxiety toward that which lies on the other side. The second challenge is this: to lead to acceptance of one's own essential limit and in its light to judge the greater or lesser weight of factual limits. In this light, narrow political boundaries could be more appropriate for a people than broader. Differing frontiers could represent the parts of a human group, linguistically but not politically united, in the group's historical essence. The acceptance of narrow boundaries could be more comprehensive in advancing the essential frontier and also the way along which a people discovers and maintains its identity. That has been demonstrated repeatedly in the course of history, and today we are in an historical moment, where the realization of the essential frontiers for most lands, at least in the Western world, depends upon their devoting themselves to more comprehensive factual frontiers.

Could there be totally comprehensive boundaries? In principle, yes! For the essential limits of all human groups are contained in the essential frontiers of humanity. The identity of every single group is a manifestation of the identity of humanity and of the nature of human existence. But the situation is different today for the factual frontiers. They are marked by one of the deepest divisions in world history, between East and West in the political sense, which includes both will to power and consciousness of calling—a consciousness of calling, indeed, which on both sides has the character of exclusiveness and therefore, given the circumstances of contemporary technology, threatens humanity with self-destruction.

IV

This leads to the deepest and most decisive of boundary line problems: all life is subject to a common frontier, finitude. The Latin, "finis," means both "frontier" and "end."

The final frontier stands behind every other frontier and gives every other the color of transitoriness. We always stand on this boundary line, but no one can cross over it. There is only one stance toward it, namely that of acceptance. That is true of individuals and of groups, families, races, nations. But nothing is more difficult than to accept the last impassable border. Everything finite would like to extend itself into infinity. The individual wants to continue his life indefinitely, and in many Christian lands a superstition has developed inside and outside the churches which misinterprets eternal life as endless duration, and does not perceive that an infinity of the finite could be a symbol for hell. In the same way, families resist their finitude in time and in space and destroy each other in a reciprocal battle to eliminate the frontier. But most important for the possibility of peace is the acceptance of their own finitude by the nations—of their time, of their space, and of the finitude of their worth.

The temptation not to accept it, to lift one's self to the level of the Unconditioned, the Divine, runs through all history. Whoever falls for this seduction destroys his world and himself. Hence the condemnations of the prophets against the peoples, above all against their own. Hence the warnings in the threnodies of the Greek choruses against the pride of the whole race. Hence the characterization which we must give the system of political absolutism of our day: namely, that they are the most terrible manifestations of the demonic-destructive powers in the depths of man. All of the Moloch-powers of the past put together do not have the sum total of sacrifices to show that have been made for them.

And again humanity stands before a devilish temptation—i.e., to turn back in one historical moment the act of creation which, across millions of years, has brought man into being. There is no human group which has the right to begin something for the sake of its frontiers whose continuation must lead to the destruction of itself and of all other human reality. To reverse the divine act of creation is a demoniacal border crossing and a revolt against the divine foundation and God-fixed goal of our being. Resistance to the attempt to set aside all limits is something else. That is necessary because he who makes a beginning must be shown that he has not become lord over the life and death of all humanity— but is himself involved in the collapse which he has occasioned.

Nothing finite can cross the frontier from finitude to infinity. But something else is possible: the Eternal can, from its side, cross over the border to the finite. It would not be the Eternal if the finite were its limit. All religions witness to this border crossing, those of which we say that they transmit law and vocation to the peoples. These are the perfecting forces from the Unlimited, the Law-establishing, the founding and leading of all being, which make peace possible. These are they which lead out of the narrows to the crossing of the frontier. These are they which give a consciousness of calling and thereby reveal the essential boundary line amidst the confusion of factual boundary lines. These are they which warn against wishing to storm the last boundary line, the frontier to the Eternal. These perfecting forces are ever there. But they can only become effective if one opens himself to them. And my wish is this for the German people, from whom I come and whom I thank for this honor, that it keep itself open, recognize its essential frontier and its calling, and fulfill progressively its factual frontiers.

~~~~~~~   *The Decline and the*

Validity of the Idea of Progress

MY SUBJECT is the idea of progress, which I will examine from
the point of view that it is valid, that it has declined very much
in its importance, and that in a new form it might be revived.
Therefore, my title is "The Decline and the Validity of the Idea
of Progress."

Let us, first, examine some basic considerations about the concepts involved. This is where my semantic critics are right. Every
discussion today in philosophy and theology demands a semantic
clearing up of the concepts which are used, because we are living
in Babylon after the tower has been destroyed and the languages
of man have been disturbed and dispersed all over the world. This
is the situation one faces today in reading theological and philosophical books. Therefore, I must guide you through some
burdensome logical, semantic, and historical journeys.

Now, first, there is a difference between the concept of progress
and the idea of progress. The concept of progress is an abstraction,
based on the description of a group of facts, of objects of observation which may well be verified or falsified; but the idea of
progress is an interpretation of existence as a whole, which means
first of all our own existence. Thus, it is a matter of decision. It
is an answer everybody has to give about the meaning of his
life. Progress as an idea is a symbol for an attitude toward our
existence. As so often in history, a concept open to logical and
empirical description and analysis has become a symbol, and in

the case of progress this is particularly true—the concept has become a symbol. What is extracted from a special realm of facts has become an expression of a general attitude toward life. Therefore, we must look at progress both as concept and as symbol. Since observation always precedes interpretation, I will give most attention to progress as a concept, because most of the confusions about progress as a symbol come from a limited and wrong analysis of progress as a concept.

Obviously progress is a universal experience which everybody has. The word is derived from *gressus* which means step, progress means stepping ahead from a less satisfactory situation to a more satisfactory situation. Imagine a lecture like this about progress, yet denying the idea of progress; someone might attempt this. But even such a person in denying the idea of progress works for progress; that is, he wants the less informed of his listeners to be better informed at the end of his lecture. In this sense, even if he speaks against the idea of progress, he accepts the concept of progress. He is implicitly progressivistic. I call this kind of thinking about progress "progressivism," which is implied in every action. Everybody who acts, acts in order to change a state of things in the direction of a better state of things. He wants to make progress. This is the most simple, the most fundamental, and actually the least contradictory way of understanding progress—the progressivism implied in every action. Nobody can get away from this. Yet this simple sense of progress is far from progress as the universal way of life, and as the law of human history. Therefore, we ask how could the idea have arisen that human history and, even preceding it, the history of all life, the history of the universe, has a progressivistic character—is progress from something lower to something higher. How could this idea develop? What are the motives behind it?

Now I must first guide you on the thorny path—especially so for Americans—of historical reminder. I hope it is a reminder because I presume that all of you know what I am referring to, but if not, be patient with me because the historical question gives the basis for the understanding of what today seems natural to us. The idea of this country is that it represents a new beginning in the history of mankind. This is true in many respects. But the new beginning is never fully new. It is always a result of preceding events, and if I may comment on my experience on two continents, I would say that Europe is endangered by its past and by all the curses coming from that past. America, on the other hand, is endangered by going ahead without looking back at the creative forces which have determined the whole of Western culture. So I wish to direct your thoughts in the first part of this paper to the past. You will discover how relevent this is to our present understanding of such an idea as that of progress.

Let us first consider the religious background of the idea of progress. The fundamental factor in this respect is prophetic religion as expressed in the Old Testament and in many forms ever since in the Christian church as well as in Judaism and Islam. It involves the idea that God has elected a nation and, later on in Christianity, people from all over the world, that he has promised something related to the future, and that in spite of all resistance on the part of the people, he will fulfill his promise. There is the vision of progress toward the future in this idea. The belief of the prophets that Yahweh, the God of Israel, will establish his heavenly rule or his kingdom over all the world is the primary basis of an interpretation of history as the place where the divine reveals itself in progress toward an end. Now this idea has always been important in the development of Christianity. There was, for example, a man whose name should be remembered, Joachim De Fiore, an abbot in Southern Italy in the twelfth century, who expressed this idea of progress in the doctrine that there were three stages in history, the stage of the Father in the Old Testament, the stage of the Son (the last thousand years of church history), and the coming or third stage of the Divine Spirit in which there will be no more church since everyone will be taught directly by the spirit. In this last stage, too, there will be equality and there will be no more marriage: history will come to an end.

Now this half-fantastic, half-realistic idea had many consequences for the whole subsequent church history, and also for this country. The idea of the third stage was taken on by the radical evangelicals in the time of the Reformation, which underlies most of this country's religion, and is seen in the idea of a revolutionary or progressivistic realization of the kingdom of God in Calvinism. It became the religious basis deep-rooted in every Western man. If you don't believe it, go to Asia—to India or Japan. I had the privilege of being in Japan for ten weeks talking everyday with Buddhist priests and scholars. There is nothing like this. "The religions of the East are of the past," I was told, "not of the future." For the religious people of the East, one wants to return to the Eternal from which one came directly, not caring for history, going out of history at some time of one's life into the desert, if possible. If you contrast this with the Western religious feeling of progressive activity, then you see what the difference is.

However, this was only the religious basis for the idea of progress. Now we come to the secular motives, and the secular elaboration of the idea of progress, which, of course, starts with the Renaissance. The man of the Renaissance is something new, not only as compared with the Middle Ages but also as compared with the late ancient world. The most important impact of the ancient world on Renaissance man was made by Stoic philosophy, but it was a transformed Stoicism. It was not the Stoicism of resignation, as it was under the Roman empire in the later Greek world, but it was the Stoicism of action. The Romans—some of the Roman emperors even—were partly mediators in this direction. However, the man of the Renaissance does not feel he is depentent on fate as the Stoics did. Rather, he feels—as expressed in painting—that when the destiny of man is compared with a sailboat, driven by the winds of contingency, man stands at the rudder and directs it. Of course, he knows that destiny gives the winds, but nevertheless, man directs destiny. This conception is unheard of in all Greek culture and is a presupposition of the idea of progress in the modern world. Out of this arose the great Renaissance Utopian writings, that is, the anticipation of a reality —*outopos*—which "has no place" in history, but which is nevertheless being expected. Such Utopias have been written ever since, into the twentieth century. It was the idea of the third stage of history, the stage of reason in bourgeois society, the stage of the classless society in the working-class movements. It was a secularized idea of the third stage, the religious foundations of which we saw. But it was not only ideas which produced this passion for purpose, it was also the social reality, the activities of bourgeois society at this time, such as the colonial extension of Europe in all directions; space extension, which has remained an element in the idea of progress up to the space exploration we are doing today; and technical extension—continuous progress in controlling nature and putting it into the service of man. All this has been based on the boundary lines of science which we have trespassed year by year since the beginning of the Renaissance up until today.

But there was another element of great importance in the idea of progress, namely the vision of nature as a progressive process from the atom to the molecule, to the cell, to the developed organism, and finally to man. This is evolution, progress in largeness of elements united in one being, with centeredness and, therefore, power being in the individual. And this line, then, was drawn beyond nature through humanity, from primitive to civilized man, to us as the representatives of the age of reason in which the potentialities of creation have come to their fulfillment.

When I tell you this, you yourself can feel how overwhelmingly impressive it is, and how virtually impossible it was to escape this idea as a symbol of faith. Progress became in the nineteenth century not only a conscious doctrine but also an unconscious dogma. When I came to this country in 1933 and spoke with students of theology, and criticized certain ideas of God, of Christ, of the Spirit, of the Church, or of sin or salvation, it didn't touch them very much but when I criticized the idea of progress, they said to me, "In what then can we believe? What do you do with our real faith?" And these were students of theology. It means that all the Christian dogmas had been transformed in the unconscious of these people (which my questions brought out) into a faith in progress. But then something happened! This dogma was shaken in the twentieth century, as foreseen by some prophetic minds in the nineteenth, first in Europe, then in America.

In Europe one of the greatest expressions of the shaking of this faith was Nietzsche's prophecy of—what unfortunately today has become a fashionable phrase—the death of God. This doesn't mean primitive, materialistic atheism; Nietzsche was far from this. But it meant the undercutting of the value-systems, Christian as well as secular, and the view of the human predicament as something in conflict, in destruction, in estrangement from true humanity.

Nietzsche was one of the predecessors of what today is called "existentialist" literature. The trend was further supported by the historical pessimism of men like Spengler, who wrote two important volumes on *The Decline of the West* in which much historical imagination was connected with much true prophecy. In the year 1916 he prophesied the coming of the period of the dictators, and in the early thirties the Communist and the Fascist dictators were a reality. The first World War and then the rise of what he prophesied of the totalitarian powers—this was the end of the belief in progress as an idea in Europe. In America it started somehow with the great economic crisis in the thirties. In Germany it started with the beginning of the Hitler period and the experience that history can fall back and that a rebarbarization can happen in any moment even in the highest culture. Then came the second World War, the cold war, and the atomic crisis. And with all this there came in this country the end of the crusading utopianism of the first third of the century. Instead, opposite Utopias appeared in literature—negative Utopias—like Huxley's *Brave New World*, or Orwell's *1984*. In many other novels and treatises the future is painted in terms of negative utopianism, in terms not of fulfillment but of dehumanization. The same can be seen in the existentialist style in the arts—whether you call it expressionist, cubist, or abstract—wherein the expression of the demonic in the underground of the individual or the group moves away from the figures and faces of human beings toward the abstract elements in the underground of reality. In philosophy there is a withdrawal into a merely formal analysis of the possibility of thinking without going into a reality itself with one's thinking. This was the end of a phase in the idea of progress, but the active motive of all our behavior cannot die, nor can the lure of future possibilities.

Today we need a new inquiry into the validity and the limits of the idea of progress. There are symptoms of reconsideration: for instance, in philosophy now there is an attempt finally to use the sharpened instruments of logical analysis to go into the real problems of human existence; and in the arts at least an attempt to use the elementary forms discovered in the last fifty years to express in a new way reality as manifestly encountered. There are other elements too: the extension of national independence; the real fight about the racial problem; and the increasing awareness, even among conservative theologians, that our attitude toward the non-Christian religions has to be one of dialogue—even the present Pope used that term. But, of course, these are symptoms and not yet fulfillments, and the threat of a relapse into the predominant pessimism (if you use that word which shouldn't be used by a philosopher) is always a danger.

We must now contribute to this reappraisal by going through a serious and perhaps painstaking analysis of the concept of progress as it appears in the different realms of life. After this somewhat dramatic historical section, I ask you to follow me through an analytic section, through an analysis of all the things one does oneself, especially in academic surroundings.

II

The tremendous force of the progressivistic idea was rooted, firstly, in observations about particular instances of progress in technical and scientific matters. But this observation was inadequate, and what is needed now is to show the non-progressive elements in reality and culture, and to demonstrate in some way how they are related to the progressive elements. There is a general principle for all this which one can follow through more fully when one thinks about these ideas. The general principle is: where there is freedom to contradict fulfillment, there the rule of progress is broken. Freedom to contradict one's fulfillment breaks the rule of the law of progress. This freedom is nothing else but another word for the moral act, which we perform every day innumerable times. There is no progress with respect to the moral act because there is no morality without free decisions, without the awareness of the power to turn with one's centered self in the one or the other direction. It means that every individual starts anew and has to make decisions for himself, whether he be on the lowest or highest level of culture or education. The German rebarbarization was looked at with great astonishment by a world which was adhering to the faith in progress. But there it was. In one of the most highly civilized nations, decisions were made by individuals and followed by many which contradicted anything we consider to be human nature and human fulfillment. This was a tremendous shock. And here is the first answer to the whole problem of progress. Every newborn infant has, when it comes to a certain point of self-awareness, the possibility of stopping progress by contradicting fulfillment in man's essential nature.

There is something else in what we usually call progress in the ethical realm, namely, coming to maturity—maturation. The child matures, and in this respect, there is progress. There is as in nature a progression from the seed to the fruit of the tree, or to the fully grown tree, but this element of maturity belongs to the individual first, and he may at any moment break out of it. We know how much this happens even in people whom we consider to be mature, and we know many who never become mature. There is something like maturing also in social groups. It means deeper understanding of man's essential nature in individual and social relations. This is not moral progress but it is cultural progress in the moral realm. It is cultural because it sees better what human nature is, but it doesn't make people better. If we had attained the full idea now of the social interrelation between the races in this country, we would be on a higher, on a more mature level; we would have deeper insight into human nature and into the content of the moral demand, but we would not have better human beings, because the goodness or not-goodness of a human being appears on all levels of culture and insight. So we can say—and this is very important for our whole consideration of this idea and for our whole culture today with respect to the free moral decisions of individuals—there are always new beginnings in the individual and sometimes in the group, but the contents can mature and can grow from one generation to another. This is the difference between civilized ethics and primitive ethics, but do not believe that on the level of primitive ethics people were worse than we are. In the smallest decisions you make in your classes, or in your homes, or wherever it may be, there is the same problem of ethical decision which is found in the crudeness of the cavemen; you are not better than they. You may be better than one of them, but one of them may be better than you. The distinction between moral decision and progress in moral content is fundamental for our judging the whole of past history.

When we look at education, we arrive at the same result. Education leads to higher cultural levels, to progress and maturity, to a production of habits of good behavior. As a consequence, education can be a kind of second nature in each of you, useful for society but, when it comes to moral freedom, you are still able to become rebarbarized, even if not openly as it was in Germany, in your personal relation to another person, to your children, your husband, your wife, or your friends. You can again start on a level which is that of freedom to contradict what you ought to be. When we add to the ordinary educational process, as we have it in a college or university, when we add to it education in psychotherapy, psychoanalysis, counselling, and all these things which are so important, what can they do? They can heal you from disturbances, they can help you to become free, but when you have been set free, let us say by successful analysis, you still have to decide. This is not moral progress; it is progress in healing, but the moral decision remains free, and now has become really free by medical or psychoanalytical help.

Besides moral freedom, the freedom of contradicting every possible instance of progress, there is a second element where there is no progress, namely, the freedom of spiritual creativity —creation in culture.

Let us look at the different cultural functions. There are the arts. Is there progress in the arts? There is progress in the technical use of materials, in the better mixing of colors, and in things like that, but is there progress in the arts? Has Homer ever been surpassed by anyone? Has Shakespeare ever been surpassed by anyone? Is an early Greek frieze worse than a classical sculpture, or is a classical worse than a modern expressionist? No. There is maturity of styles; there are good and bad representatives of style, but you cannot compare artistic styles in terms of progress. A style starts, often very modestly and preliminarily. It grows, it becomes mature, it produces its greatest expressions, then it decays. But there is no progress from one style to another. There is no progress from the Gothic to the Classical style. (And this needs to be said against our Gothic church buildings—we shouldn't pretend that we can go back to the Gothic style, after our modern stylistic feelings and developmental possibilities have become so

73

different.) So, creativity in the arts admits of maturity, admits of "great moments"—*kairoi*—right times, decisive times, turning points, all this, but it does not admit progress from one style to another.

The same is true in the realm of knowledge. If you look at philosophy, you see an analytic element in our great philosophers as well as a visionary element. Take Aristotle, for example, who unites both of them so clearly. In every kind of knowledge a philosophical element is present. You can also speak of a logical and empirical element in knowledge which is detached and necessary, and an existentialist and inspirational element which is involved. Both are there, and the very fact that in all great philosophers there was this visionary, involved, inspirational element makes it impossible to speak about progress in the history of philosophy except in those elements which are connected with a sharpened logical analysis or a tremendous increase in empirical knowledge. I have never found a philosopher who I could say progressed over Parmenides the Eleatic of the sixth century B.C. Of course, there is much more empirical knowledge, there is much more refined analysis, but the vision of this man, and of Heraclitus, his polar friend and opposite, cannot be surpassed. There is no qualitative progress from Heraclitus to Whitehead.

And there is no progress in humanity, that is, in the formation of the individual person. I was struck by this once when I saw a photograph of an old Sumerian sculpture, perhaps of a priestess, and looking at it said to myself, "Look at the sculptures and paintings of great representatives of humanity in the following history of three or four thousand years." I found no progress at all. I found differences, but I didn't find progress. This means that even justice as well as humanity are not matters of progress except in technical elements. If I think, for instance, of democracy there is progress in largeness of the number of people involved, and progress in maturity in some respects, but there was justice in the state of Athens, justice in old Israel, in Rome, in the Middle Ages, and there is justice in modern democracy. The progress is quantitative, but the quality of the ideas of humanity and justice has not progressed.

Now I come to the most difficult problem—progress in religion. Of course, it is simple if you follow the conservative or fundamentalist idea that there is one true religion and many false ones. Then, needless to say, there is no progress. But even if you hold this view, you have a difficulty, namely, the Old Testament— what about that? Isn't there something then like progress—progressive revelation? So the problem appears even in Christianity. There is development, there is progress. Even in church history there is supposed to be progress according to the Gospel of John where Jesus is reported to have said that the Spirit will introduce you into all truth. This is progress. Furthermore, there are Christian theologies which expect new revelations even beyond Jesus the Christ. This, of course, would be post-Christian religion. Now if we look at this, we encounter great difficulties. On the one hand, Christianity claims that there is no possible progress beyond what is given in Jesus the Christ; on the other hand, there is great progress in world history in many respects—in knowledge as well as in other areas. How shall we deal with this problem?

Here is where religion might provide the standpoint from which we might understand the whole problem better. I would say that we must replace the idea of progress by two other concepts: the concept of maturing, and the concept of "the decisive moment." What we need is an understanding of history in which there are two things, rather than a single, continuous line of progress. (I hope that what I have said about all the other realms—the ethical, the cultural, the artistic, the scientific, the philosophical, the religious—showed this clearly.) "Great moments" or, if you want to accept the term I like very much, taken from the New Testament or from classical Greek, the term *kairos*, the right time, fulfilled time, time in which something decisive happens, is not the same as *chronos*, chronological time, which is watch time, but it means the qualitative time in which "something happens." I would say, therefore, that in history we have two processes, not progress as a universal event, but the maturing of potentialities, the maturing of a style, for instance, or the maturing in the education of a human being. It is not progress beyond this human being. He or she may give something to their children, but children must decide again on their own. There is no progress; they must start anew. Two things then we can see in history. One is the process of maturing in terms of potentialities; the other is the great moments, the *kairoi*, in history in which something new happens. However, that new thing which happens is not in a progressivistic line with the other new things before and after it. This is only true in the technical and scientific realm so far as the logical elements are implied, but it is not so in the realm of spiritual creativity and of the moral act.

My description and analysis of progress has been more careful than is usual, but I believe that the service an academic lecturer can give is to show his listeners where the problems lie, and to steer them away from the popular talk about such weighty problems. This I have tried to do, and now perhaps we will have some of the fruits of this. When progress is elevated into a symbol or an idea, as I said in the beginning, then it can take on two forms. The one is the idea of endless progress, without a limit, in which one moves further and further along, and things get better and better. The other is the Utopian form, which is historically much more important; namely, that at some point in time man's essential nature will be fulfilled. What is possible for man will then exist. Now, what happens with these two? In the first type, progress runs ahead without aim, unless progress itself is taken to be the aim, but there is no goal at the end of the progression. Thus, it is simply a matter of going ahead, and of course, if my analysis before was right, this is possible to a certain extent in the technical and scientific realms. But it is not possible in the realms where vision and inspiration play a role. The other type, the Utopian, has produced all the tremendous passions in history for it is the principle of revolution. However, after the revolution is successful, the great disappointment follows, and this disappointment produces cynicism and sometimes complete withdrawal from history. We have it in some forms of Christianity—we have it strongly in Lutheranism and in the Greek Orthodox Church; we have it less in Calinism and Evangelical radicalism, which underlies this country; and we have it in an anti-Christian way as a result of the terrible experiences of suffering in Asiatic religions, especially in Buddhism with its withdrawal from history.

Now the question is, is there a way of avoiding the Utopianism which sees the fullfillment of history around the corner; which says, only one step more and we will be in the classless society; only one step more and we will be an educated nation; only one step more and all our youngsters will reach full humanity, or all our social groups will stand for true justice. If only all men of good will—that means we—stand together, everything will be all right. All this is Utopianism. In contrast, I want to save you, by my criticism of the idea of progress, from the cynical consequences of disappointed Utopianism. In my long life I have experienced the breakdown of the Utopianism of the Western intelligentsia both in Europe and America and the tremendous cynicism and despair which followed it and, finally, the emptiness of not being ultimately concerned about anything. Therefore, I think that we must put something else in place of these two types of progressivism. Endless progress may be symbolized by running ahead indefinitely into an empty space. We will do that, but it is not the meaning of life; nor are better and better gadgets the meaning of life. What is the meaning of life then? Perhaps it is something else. Perhaps there are great moments in history. There is in these great moments not total fulfillment but there is the victory over a particular power of destruction, a victory over a demonic power which was creative and now has become destructive. This is a possibility, but don't expect that it *must* happen. It might not happen; that is a continuous threat hanging over development in history. But there *may* be a *kairos*.

After the first World War in Germany, we believed, just because of the defeat of Germany, that there was a *kairos*, a great moment, in which something new could be created. In this sense we were progressive, but we did not believe that it was necessary that this would happen. Inevitable progress should not be sought by us, for there is no such thing. Of course, what we hoped for then was completely destroyed by the Hitler movement. Out of these experiences we came to see that there is a possibility of victory over a particular demonic power—a particular force of destruction—or to put it simply, there is a possibility of solving a particular problem, as for instance, the race problem in our time. But even if this does happen, it doesn't mean inevitable progress. We must fight for it, and we may be defeated, but even if not, new demonic powers will arise.

There is a wonderful symbolism in the last book of the Bible, in the idea of the thousand years' rule of Christ in history. In these thousand years, which is a symbolic number, of course, the demonic forces will be banned—put into chains in the underworld. This is all symbolism. But they are not annihilated and they may come to the surface again, as they will in the final struggle. When we thought about our problems after the first World War, we used this symbol—not in its literal sense, of course—as expressing the awareness that you can ban a particular demonic force. Hitler was banned, but the powers behind Hitler, the demonic forces in mankind and in every individual are not definitely annihilated; they are banned for a moment and they may return again. So instead of a progressivistic, Utopian, or empty vision of history, let us think of the great moments for which we must keep ourselves open, and in which the struggle of the divine and the demonic in history may be decided for one moment for the divine against the demonic, though there is no guarantee that this will happen. On the contrary, in the view of the Bible, especially the book of Revelation, the growth of the divine powers in history are contradicted by a growth of the demonic powers.

So in every moment the fight is going on and the only thing

we can say is this: If there is a new beginning, let us mature in it; if there is a new beginning in world history as we have it now in this country and beyond this country, let us follow it and develop it to its maturity. But let us not look at history in the sense of progress which will be going on and finally come to an end which is wonderful and fulfilling. There is no such thing in history, because man is free, free to contradict his own essential nature and his own fulfillment. As a Christian theologian I would say that fulfillment is going on in every moment here and now beyond history, not some time in the future, but here and now above ourselves. When I have to apply this to a meeting like this, then I would say it might well be that in such a meeting in the inner movements of some of us, something might happen which is elevated out of time into eternity. This then is a non-Utopian and a true fulfillment of the meaning of history and of our own individual life.

~~~~~~~~ *The Significance of the History*

of Religions for the Systematic Theologian

In this lecture, I wish to deal with three basic considerations. I call the first one "two basic decisions." A theologian who accepts the subject, "The Significance of the History of Religions for the Systematic Theologian," and takes this subject seriously, has already made, explicitly or implicitly, two basic decisions. On the one hand he has separated himself from a theology which rejects all religions other than that of which he is a theologian. On the other hand if one accepts the subject affirmatively and seriously, he has rejected the paradox of a religion of non-religion, or a theology without theos, also called a theology of the secular.

Both of these attitudes have a long history. The former has been renewed in our century by Karl Barth. The latter is now most sharply expressed in the so-called theology-without-God language. For the former attitude, either the one religion is *vera religio*, true religion, against all others which are *religiones falsâe*, false religions, or as it is expressed in modern terms, one's own religion is revelation, but the other religion is only a futile human attempt to reach God. This becomes the definition of all religion—a futile human attempt to reach God.

Therefore, from this point of view it is not worthwhile to go into the concrete differences of the religions. I remember the half-hearted way in which, for instance, Emil Brunner did it. I recall the theological isolation of historians of religion like my very highly esteemed friend, the late Rudolf Otto, and even today the similar situation of a man like Friedrich Heiler. Also one recalls the bitter attacks on Schleiermacher for his use of the concept of religion for Christianity. I remember the attacks on my views when for the first time (forty years ago) I gave a seminar on Schleiermacher at Marburg. Such an approach was considered a crime at that time.

In order to reject both this old and new orthodox attitude, one must accept the following systematic presuppositions. First, one must say that revelatory experiences are universally human. Religions are based on something that is given to a man where-ever he lives. He is given a revelation, a particular kind of ex-perience which always implies saving powers. One never can separate revelation and salvation. There are revealing and saving powers in all religions. God has not left himself unwitnessed. This is the first presupposition.

The second assumption states that revelation is received by man in terms of his finite human situation. Man is biologically, psychologically, and sociologically limited. Revelation is received under the conditions of man's estranged character. It is received always in a distorted form, especially if religion is used as a means to an end and not as an end in itself.

There is a third presupposition that one must accept. When systematic theologians assume the significance of the history of religions, it involves the belief that there are not only particular revelatory experiences throughout human history, but that there is a revelatory process in which the limits of adaptation and the failures of distortion are subjected to criticism. Such criticism takes three forms: the mystical, the prophetic, and the secular.

A fourth assumption is that there may be—and I stress this, there *may* be—a central event in the history of religions which unites the positive results of those critical developments in the history of religion in and under which revelatory experiences are going on—an event which, therefore, makes possible a concrete theology that has universalistic significance.

There is also a fifth presupposition. The history of religions in its essential nature does not exist alongside the history of culture. The sacred does not lie beside the secular, but it is its depths. The sacred is the creative ground and at the same time a critical judgment of the secular. But the religious can be this only if it is at the same time a judgment on itself, a judgment which must use the secular as a tool of one's own religious self-criticism.

Only if the theologian is willing to accept these five presuppositions can he seriously and fully affirm the significance of the history of religions for theology against those who reject such significance in the name of a new or of an old absolutism.

On the other hand, he who accepts the significance of the history of religion must stand against the no-God-language theology. He must reject also the exclusive emphasis on the secular or the idea that the sacred has, so to speak, been fully absorbed by the secular.

The last of the five points, the point about the relation of the sacred and the secular, has already reduced the threat of the "God is dead" oracle. Religion must use the secular as a critical tool against itself, but the decisive question is: *Why any religions at all?* Here one means religions in the sense of a realm of symbols, rites, and institutions. Can they not be neglected by a secular theologian in the same way he probably neglects the history of magic or of astrology? If he has no use for the idea of God, what can bring him to attribute high significance to the history of religion?

In order to affirm religion against the attack from this side, the theologian must have one basic presupposition. He must assume that religion as a structure of symbols of intuition and action—that means myths and rites within a social group—has lasting necessity for any, even the most secularized culture and the most demythologized theology. I derive this necessity, the lasting necessity of religion, from the fact that spirit requires embodiment in order to become real and effective. It is quite well to say that the Holy, or the Ultimate, or the Word is within the secular realm and I myself have done so innumerable times. But in order to say that something is *in* something, it must have at least a possibility to be *outside* of it. In other words, that which is *in* and that *in* which it is, must be distinguishable. In some way their manifestations must differ. And this is the question: *In what does the merely secular differ from that secular which would be the object of a secular theology?*

Let me say the same thing in a well known, popular form. The reformers were right when they said that every day is the Lord's Day and, therefore, they devaluated the sacredness of the seventh day. But in order to say this, there must have been a Lord's Day, and that not only once upon a time but continuously in counterbalance against the overwhelming weight of the secular. This is what makes God–language necessary, however untraditional that language may be. This makes a serious affirmation of the history of religion possible.

Therefore, as theologians, we have to break through two barriers against a free approach to the history of religions: the orthodox–exclusive one and the secular–rejective one. The mere term "religion" still produces a flood of problems for the systematic theologian, and this is increased by the fact that the two fronts of resistance, though coming from opposite sides, involve an alliance. This has happened and *still* happens.

Both sides are reductionistic, and both are inclined to eliminate everything from Christianity except the figure of Jesus of Nazareth. The neo-orthodox group does this by making him the exclusive place where the word of revelation can be heard. The secular group does the same things by making him the representative of a theologically relevant secularity. But this can be done only if the picture and message of Jesus is itself drastically reduced. He must be limited to an embodiment of the ethical call, especially in the social direction, and this is then the only thing which is left of the whole message of the Christ. In *this* case, of course, history of religion is not needed any longer, not even the Jewish and Christian. Therefore, in order to have a valued, evaluated, and significant understanding of the history of religions, one has to break through the Jesus–centered alliance of the opposite poles, the orthodox as well as the secular.

Now I come to my second consideration: a theology of the history of religions. The traditional view of the history of religions is limited to that history as it is told in the Old and New Testament, and enlarged to include church history as the continuity of that history. Other religions are not qualitatively distinguished from each other. They all are perversions of a kind of original revelation but without particular revelatory experiences of any value for Christian theology. They are pagan religions, religions of the nations, but they are not bearers of revelation and salvation. Actually, this principle was never fully carried through. Jews and Christians were both influenced religiously by the religions of conquered and conquering nations, and frequently these religions almost suffocated Judaism and Christianity and led to explosive reactions in both of them.

Therefore, what we need, if we want to accept the title of this lecture, "The Significance of the History of Religions for the Systematic Theologian," is a theology of the history of religions in which the positive valuation of universal revelation balances the critical one. Both are necessary. This theology of the history of religions can help systematic theologians to understand the present moment and the nature of our own historical place, both in the particular character of Christianity and in its universal claim.

I am still grateful, looking back to my own formative period of study and the time after it, to what in German is called the *religionsgeschichtliche Schule*, the School of History of Religions in biblical and church historical studies. These studies opened our eyes and demonstrated the degree to which the biblical tradition participates in the Asia Minor and Mediterranean traditions. I remember the liberating effect of the understanding of universal, human motives in the stories of Genesis, or in Hellenistic existentialism and in Persian eschatology as they appeared in the late periods of the Old and New Testament.

From this point of view, all the history of religions produced symbols for savior figures which then supplied the framework for the New Testament understanding of Jesus and his work. This was liberating. These things did not fall from heaven like stones, but there was a long preparatory revelatory history which finally, in the *kairos*, in the right time, in the fulfilled time, made possible the appearance of Jesus as the Christ. All this was done without hurting the uniqueness of the prophetic attack on religion in the Old Testament and of the unique power of Jesus in the New Testament. Later on, in my own development, as in that of many other theologians, the significance was made clear both of the religions which surrounded the Old and New Testament situation, and the importance of religions farther removed from Biblical history.

The first question confronting a theology of the history of Israel and of the Christian Church is the history of salvation, but the history of salvation is something within the history. It is expressed in great symbolic moments, in *kairoi* such as the various efforts at reform in the history of the Church. In the same way, nobody would identify history of religions and history of salvation, or revelation, but one searches for symbolic moments. If the history of religions is taken seriously, are there *kairoi* in the general history of religions? Attempts have been made to find such *kairoi*. There was the enlightenment of the eighteenth century. Everything for these theologians was a preparation for the great *kairos*, the great moment, in which mature reason is reached in mankind. There are still religious elements in this reason: God, freedom, immortality. Kant developed it in his famous book, *Religion Within the Limits of Pure Reason*.

Another attempt was the romanticist understanding of history which led to Hegel's famous effort. From his point of view, there is a progressive history of religion. It progresses according to the basic philosophical categories which give the structure of all reality. Christianity is the highest and last point, and it is called "revealed religion," but this Christianity is philosophically demythologized. Such a view is a combination of Kantian philosophy and the message of the New Testament.

All earlier religions in Hegel's construction of the history of religions are *aufgehoben*, which can only be translated by two English words, namely, "taken in" and "removed." In this way, therefore, that which is past in the history of religion has lost its meaning. It is only an element in the later development. This means, for instance, that for Hegel the Indian religions are long, long past, long ago finished, and have no contemporary meaning. They belong to an early stage of history. Hegel's attempt to develop a theology of the history of religion resulted in the experiential theology which was very strong in America about thirty years ago. It was based on the idea of remaining open to new experiences of religious character in the future. Today men like Toynbee point in this direction—or perhaps look for that in religious experience which leads to a union of the great religions. In any case, it is a post-Christian era that is looking for such a construction.

It is necessary to mention also Teilhard de Chardin who stresses the development of a universal, divine-centered consciousness which is basically Christian. Christianity takes in all spiritual elements of the future. I am dissatisfied with such an attempt. I am also dissatisfied with my own, but I will give it in order to induce you to try yourself because that is what one should do if he takes the history of religions seriously.

My approach is dynamic-typological. There is no progressive development which goes on and on, but there are elements in the experience of the Holy which are always there, if the Holy is experienced. These elements, if they are predominant in one religion create a particular religious type. It is necessary to go into greater depth, but I will only mention a tentative scheme which would appear this way. The universal religious basis is the experience of the Holy within the finite. Universally in everything finite and particular, or in this and that finite, the Holy appears in a special way. I could call this the sacramental basis of all religions—the Holy here and now which can be seen, heard, dealt with, in spite of its mysterious character. We still have remnants of this in the highest religions, in their sacraments, and I believe that without it, a religious group would become an association of moral clubs, as much of Protestantism is, because it has lost the sacramental basis.

Then, there is a second element, namely a critical movement against the demonization of the sacramental, making it into an object which can be handled. This element is embodied in various critical ways. The first of these critical movements is mystical. This mystical movement means that one is not satisfied with any of the concrete expressions of the Ultimate, of the Holy. One goes beyond them. Man goes to the one beyond any manifoldness. The Holy as the Ultimate lies beyond any of its embodiments. The embodiments are justified. They are accepted but they are secondary. One must go beyond them in order to reach the highest, the Ultimate itself. The particular is denied for the Ultimate One. The concrete is devaluated.

Another element, or the third element in the religious experience, is the element of "ought to be." This is the ethical or prophetic element. Here the sacramental is criticized because of demonic consequences like the denial of justice in the name of holiness. This is the whole fight of the Jewish prophets against sacramental religion. In some of the words of Amos and Hosea this is carried so far that the whole cult is abrogated. This criticism of the sacramental basis is decisive for Judaism and is one element in Christianity. But again I would say, if this is without the sacramental and the mystical element, then it becomes moralistic and finally secular.

I would like to describe the unity of these three elements in a religion which one could call—I hesitate to do so, but I don't know a better word—"The Religion of the Concrete Spirit." And it might well be that one can say the inner *telos*, which means the inner aim of a thing, such as the *telos* of the acorn is to become a tree—the inner aim of the history of religions is to become a Religion of the Concrete Spirit. But we cannot identify this Religion of the Concrete Spirit with any actual religion, not even Christianity as a religion. But I would dare to say, of course, dare as a Protestant theologian, that I believe that there is no higher expression for what I call the synthesis of these three elements than in Paul's doctrine of the Spirit. There we have the two fundamental elements: the ecstatic and the rational element united. There is ecstasy but the highest creation of the ecstasy is love in the sense of *agape*. There is ecstasy but the other creation of ecstasy is *gnosis*, the knowledge of God. It is knowledge, and it is not disorder and chaos.

The positive and negative relation of these elements or motives now gives the history of religions its dynamic character. The inner *telos* of which I spoke, the Religion of the Concrete Spirit, is, so to speak, that toward which everything drives. But we cannot say that this is a merely futuristic expectation. It appears everywhere in the struggle against the demonic resistance of the sacramental basis and the demonic and secularistic distortion of the critics of the sacramental basis. It appears in a fragmentary way in many moments in the history of religions. Therefore, we have to absorb the past history of religions, and annihilate it in this way, but we have a genuine living tradition consisting in the moments in which this great synthesis became, in a fragmentary way, reality. We can see the whole history of religions in this sense as a fight for the Religion of the Concrete Spirit, a fight of God against religion within religion. And this phrase, the fight of God within religion against religion, could become the key for understanding the otherwise extremely chaotic, or at least seemingly chaotic, history of religions.

Now, as Christians we see in the appearance of Jesus as the Christ the decisive victory in this struggle. There is an old symbol for the Christ, Christus Victor, and this can be used again in this view of the history of religions. And so it is already connected in the New Testament with the victory over the demonic powers and the astrological forces. It points to the victory on the cross as a negation of any demonic claim. And I believe we see here immediately that this can give us a Christological approach which could liberate us from many of the dead ends into which the discussion of the Christological dogma has led the Christian churches from the very beginning. In this way, the continuation of critical moments in history, of moments of *kairoi* in which the Religion of the Concrete Spirit is actualized fragmentarily can happen here and there.

The criterion for us as Christians is the event of the cross. That which has happened there in a symbolic way, which gives the criterion, also happens fragmentarily in other places, in other moments, has happened and will happen even though they are not historically or empirically connected with the cross.

Now I come to a question which was very much in the center of this whole conference, namely, how these dynamics of the history of religions are related to the relationship of the religious and of the secular. The holy is not only open to demonization and to the fight of God against religion as a fight against the demonic implications of religion. But the holy is also open to secularization. And these two, demonization and secularization, are related to each other insofar as secularization is the third and most radical form of de-demonization. Now, this is a very important systematic idea.

You know the meaning of the term, profane, "to be before the doors of the sanctuary," and the meaning of secular, "belonging to the world." In both cases, somebody leaves the ecstatic, mysterious fear of the Holy for the world of ordinary rational structures. It would be easy to fight against this, to keep the people in the sanctuary if the secular had not been given critical religious function by itself. And this makes the problem so serious. The secular is the rational and the rational must judge the irrationality of the Holy. It must judge its demonization.

The rational structure of which I am speaking implies the

moral, the legal, the cognitive and the aesthetic. The consecration of life which the Holy gives is at the same time the domination of life by the ecstatic forms of the Holy, and the repression of the intrinsic demands of goodness, of justice, of truth and of beauty. Secularization occuring in such a context is liberation.

In this sense, both the prophets and the mystics were predecessors of the secular. The Holy became slowly the morally good, or the philosophically true, and later the scientifically true, or the aesthetically expressive. But then, a profound dialectic appears. The secular shows its inability to live by itself. The secular which is right in fighting against the domination by the Holy, becomes empty and becomes victim of what I call "quasi-religions." And these "quasi-religions" imply an oppressiveness like the demonic elements of the religions. But they are worse, as we have seen in our century, because they are without the depths and the richness of the genuine religious traditions.

And here, another *telos*, the inner aim of the history of religions, appears. I call it *theonomy* from *theos*—God and *nomos* —law. If the autonomous forces of knowledge, of aesthetics, of law and morals point to the ultimate meaning of life, then we have theonomy. Then they are not dominated, but in their inner being they point beyond themselves to the Ultimate. In reality, there takes place another dynamic struggle, namely, between a consecration of life, which becomes heteronomous and a self-actualization of all the cultural functions, which becomes autonomous and empty.

Theonomy appears in what I called "the Religion of the Concrete Spirit" in fragments, never fully. Its fulfillment is eschatological, its end is expectation which goes beyond time to eternity. This theonomous element in the relation of the sacred and the secular is an element in the structure of the Religion of the Concrete Spirit. It is certainly progressive, as every action is. Even to give a lecture has in itself the tendency to make progress in some direction, but it is not progressivistic—it doesn't imagine a temporal fulfillment once upon a time. And here I differ from Teilhard de Chardin to whom I feel very near in so many respects.

And now my third and last consideration: the interpretation of the theological tradition in the light of religious phenomena. Let me tell you about a great colleague, a much older colleague at the University of Berlin, Adolph Harnack. He once said that Christianity in its history embraces all elements of the history of religions. This was a partially true insight, but he did not follow it through. He did not see that if this is so, then there must be a much more positive relationship between the whole history of religion and the history of the Christian Church. And so, he narrowed down his own constructive theology to a kind of high bourgeois, individualistic, moralistic theology.

I now want to return my thanks on this point to my friend Professor Eliade for the two years of seminars and the cooperation we had in them. In these seminars I experienced that every individual doctrinal statement or ritual expression of Christianity receives a new intensity of meaning. And, in terms of a kind of an apologia yet also a self-accusation, I must say that my own *Systematic Theology* was written before these seminars and had another intention, namely, the apologetic discussion against and with the secular. Its purpose was the discussion or the answering of questions coming from the scientific and philosophical criticism of Christianity. But perhaps we need a longer, more intensive period of interpenetration of systematic theological study and religious historical studies. Under such circumstances the structure of religious thought might develop in connection with another or different fragmentary manifestation of theonomy or of the Religion of the Concrete Spirit. This is my hope for the future of theology.

To see this possibility one should look to the example of the emphasis on the particular which the method of the history of religions gives to the systematic theologian. It is to be seen in two negations: against a supranatural and against a natural theology. First, one sees this in supranatural theology which was the way classical Protestant orthodoxy formulated the idea of God in systematic theology. This concept of God appears in revelatory documents which are inspired but were not prepared for in history. For orthodoxy these views are found in the biblical books, or for Islam in the Koran. From there, dogmatic statements are prepared out of the material of the holy books by the Church, usually in connection with doctrinal struggles, formulated in creeds or official collections of doctrines, and theologically explained with the help of philosophy. All this was done without looking beyond the revelatory circle which one calls one's own religion or faith. This is the predominant method in all Christian churches.

Then there is the method of natural theology, the philosophical derivation of religious concepts from an analysis of reality encountered as a whole, and especially from an analysis of the structure of the human mind. Often these concepts, God and others, are then related to traditional doctrines; sometimes they are not related.

These are the two main methods traditionally used. The method of the history of religions takes the following steps: first, it uses the material of the tradition as existentially experienced by those who work theologically. But since one works theologically, he must also have the detachment which is necessary to observe any reality. This is the first step.

In the second step, the historian of religions takes over from the naturalistic methodology the analysis of mind and reality to show where the religious question is situated in human experiences both within ourselves and within our world. For instance, the experience of finitude, the experience of concern about the meaning of our being, the experience of the Holy as Holy, and so on.

Then the third step is to present a phenomenology of religion, showing the phenomena, especially that which shows itself in the history of religion—the symbols, the rites, the ideas, and the various activities. Then the fourth step consists in the attempt to point out the relation of these phenomena—their relatedness, their difference, their contradictions—to the traditional concepts and to the problems that emerge from this. Finally, the historian of religions tries to place the reinterpreted concepts into the framework of the dynamics of religious and of secular history and especially into the framework of our present religious and cultural situation. Now these five steps include part of the earlier methods but they introduce that which was done by the earlier method into the context of the history of the human race and into the experiences of mankind as expressed in the great symbols of religious history.

The last point, namely, putting everything into the present situation leads to another advantage, or if you wish to call it so, to a new element of truth. This provides the possibility of understanding religious symbols in relation to the social matrix within which they have grown and into which we have to reintroduce them today. This is an exceedingly important step. Religious symbols are not stones falling from heaven. They have their roots in the totality of human experience including local surroundings, in all their ramifications, both political and economic. And these symbols then can be understood partly as in revolt against them. And in both cases, this is very important for our way of using symbols and reintroducing them.

A second positive consequence of this method is that we can use religious symbolism as a language of the doctrine of man, as the language of anthropology, not in the empirical sense of this word, but in the sense of doctrine of man—man in his true nature. The religious symbols say something to us about the way in which men have understood themselves in their very nature. The discussion about the emphasis on sin in Christianity and the lack of such emphasis in Islam is a good example. This shows a fundamental difference in the self-interpretation of two great religions and cultures, of men as men. And in this way, we enlarge our understanding of the nature of man in a way which is more embracing than any particular technical psychology. But now my last word. What does this mean for our relationship to the religion of which one is a theologian? Such a theology remains rooted in its experiential basis. Without this, no theology at all is possible. But it tries to formulate the basic experiences which are universally valid in universally valid statements. The universality of a religious statement does not lie in an all-embracing abstraction which would destroy religion as such, but it lies in the depths of every concrete religion. Above all it lies in the openness to spiritual freedom both from one's own foundation and for one's own foundation.